The Art Of Manipulation

Influence Whoever Stands Before You and Learn the Right Mindset to Face Life and People Thanks to the Psychology of Persuasion

[Anthony Secrets]

Table of Contents

INTRODUCTION 1

The Art of Manipulation......6

CHAPTER 1: Practical "xy" technique to influence even a Head of State (used by the secret services) 15

Be Aware of Your BATNA......19

CHAPTER 2: Achieve your goals thanks to the psychology of persuasion......25

CHAPTER 3: Mindset 3%: understand the mental patterns of 3% of the world population and reach success too!......58

CHAPTER 4: Technique of fear: use it to make anyone do what you want......69

How To Use The Technique......86

CHAPTER 5: Mental manipulation in everyday life: best secrets 88

Fatigue Inducement 89

How To Use The Technique......90

Choice Restriction 91

How To Use The Technique......92

Subliminal Influence......93

Techniques of Manipulation 94

CHAPTER 6: 10 best mental manipulation techniques used on prisoners of war......109

People easily open up to you 110

You resolve conflicts easily 111

You easily turn into a leader 111

You can work anywhere, with anyone 111

You get yourself a high-paid job easily 112

You don't carry out or say things you later regret 112

You are a valued friend and confidant 113

You are fulfilled 113

Self-awareness 113

Social skills 114

Emotional regulation 114

CHAPTER 7: How to recognize the manipulation in the sale: best tricks 115

CHAPTER 8: In-depth analysis of a politician: how do they manipulate us? 130

CHAPTER 9: Take control of your life and manipulate whoever you want 134

CONCLUSION 141

INTRODUCTION

The process of leading another to make certain decisions is really what this is about. There are many areas in life where this is not only beneficial but necessary. We don't realize what is taking place in these areas because of it being so common. An example is a lawyer in the courtroom. That lawyer's job is to manipulate, or rather persuade, 12 people to make a common decision. Politicians are always practicing persuasion. Teachers do this and so do parents. It's happening all the time and all around us. However, unless it is malicious in nature, it goes unnoticed.

Here is the perfect place for this piece of advice. Just as the definition says, there are insidious reasons why some choose to manipulate. This isn't always true, but it happens. There are people with harmful or malicious intentions and the outcomes with manipulation will match the intentions of those who practice it. In this book, we will discuss both the good and the bad. There will be examples given for each. On a personal note, I believe there to be no personal advantage worthy of harm to others. If you, the reader, see this differently,

I strongly encourage you to do some soul searching before going on with the reading. Karma is real and is vengeful. There are many people with this testimony.

On the other side of this token, there are real and genuine benefits to this art which can lead to excellent outcomes. Just as with any other talent or ability, use it wisely and in the best ways possible and you will reap positive benefits. You can become very successful, in any endeavor you choose, without harming anyone in the process. You can even use manipulation of others to benefit those whom you are controlling, or guiding, at the time. Manipulate someone in order to lead that person to help him or herself. That will bring fantastic rewards and positive Karma.

There is one big difference between manipulating someone and persuading them. This is the intentions of the person doing it. If you are trying to make someone do a certain thing, or make a certain decision, and you know that it will be what is best for both of you, you are persuading that person. If you are doing it knowing that it is only going to benefit you and may actually harm the other, you are manipulating. One of them is bad and the other isn't. The will and intentions of the person trying to lead the other will probably match his or her character. In saying this, it's meant to assume that bad people will manipulate while good people persuade.

Everywhere we look we can see persuasion taking place. There are a few primary areas for sure, but it's happening almost everywhere in some form. The most obvious areas are sales, schools, and things such as political campaigns. However, life and society are filled with persuasions. Don't think so? Have you ever heard of peer-pressure? If you went to any school, you know what this is. We don't need to be persuaded by a certain person other than ourselves. We allow ourselves to be manipulated by those around us every day and this is done without them even knowing it!

People are persuaded to wear certain kinds of clothing, listen to certain music, support certain sports teams, and the list goes on and on. Almost all of the time, we make our choices based on persuasion, or even manipulation, in some part. When we were teenagers, we had to wear a specific brand of shoes because that's what our friends were wearing. It was uncool to go against the status quo with things like that. If most of our friends were Dallas Cowboys fans, more than likely, we were too. If most of your friends listened to a specific genre of music, you probably did the same. They were not the ones persuading you. You did it to yourself by their influences. If all of this didn't happen to you, you were probably seen as an outcast or homeschooled.

As you grew into a young teenager, you probably knew exactly what to say to your parents in order to get something. Hopefully, it wasn't something bad and you were not a malicious and deviant manipulator, but you knew just want to say. You knew which strings to pull so that you would get your way. You were manipulating your parents by doing this. If you didn't, bless your heart and your parents should be extremely proud. The rest of us, from time to time, did these things.

How about when you go to buy anything where there is someone to assist you in your purchase? Salespeople are not there to manipulate. They are there for persuasion. Good salespeople know exactly what to say, how to look and act, and which ways they can lead you specifically to make a purchase. They will look at you, ask you a few questions about yourself, and from there can take off with many different persuasion techniques. This isn't just real-estate agents and car salesmen but includes many different kinds of sales.

Your teachers, all the way from pre-school to graduate school, are there to persuade you. Good teachers are also good manipulators, or good at persuasion. A good teacher must be able to educate you while keeping your attention and making learning fun and enjoyable. They should make the students feel involved in the learning process and allow students to participate and be able to speak what they think. Learning isn't simply one person giving another information but should be a two-way process. Kids who feel like they have some say and less like they are just told what to do all of the time, respond much better to teachers and those with authority. People want to matter and kids are no different.

With the ability to successfully manipulate others, comes the responsibility of controlling what you do and how it's done. It's like the old saying, "with power comes responsibility." Ideally, this is the case and should always be made to be true. We see exceptions daily but should ignore poor examples like that. With any other unique ability, a person may possess, it should be used for the betterment of the world and society and not be used selfishly.

With that information in the bag, let's begin our journey into the world of mind-control and manipulation. There are going to be some dry areas in the reading. The book Gods require this from time to time. However, most will be very lighthearted, informative, and enjoyable to read. So, without further ado, let's get to reading and let the learning begin!

The Art of Manipulation

Generally, manipulation refers to the act of regulating somebody for your benefit, often fraudulently. The art of manipulation does not have to necessarily involve making people act the way you want them to, but it rather entails causing them to want to react the way you desire them to.

There are several ways you can use to get people to proceed the way you desire or require them to. You have to know their true yearnings, then reverse this towards the goal you want to achieve. Manipulation is more of a psychological scheme since it aims at changing the thought process of an individual through indirect and underhanded tactics. If the manipulator advances his or her interests, then such tactics are considered as manipulative and devious.

The handier the person is to you, the more stress-free it is to manipulate them. In most cases, your romantic partners are the best people to use when testing your manipulation skills. Controlling someone, and if it feels like a bad word; persuading someone, involves making someone feel like it was their decision all along.

It has been established that men are easily manipulated through mastery and the individuality accompanying improvement since all they want is perfectionism. On the other hand, women tend to have balanced life relationships with their families and friends. Therefore, overpowering influences on precise interactions create a scorching longing to bring it up. In simple terms, this means that while women lean towards balance, men lean towards their emphasis on fastidiousness.

When manipulating someone, most individuals opt for the short term, but the real art of manipulation entails being affectionate about the long-term game. You need to be patient and make the persuasion look natural just like a professional, and the persuasiveness should flow without requiring loads of efforts. This forbearance helps in incapacitating the intellectual barriers that eventually helps you to have the right mindset.

There are several factors that motivate people to opt for manipulations. Some of them include (though are not limited to):

- The want to improve someone's gains and goals at the cost of others.
- A strong feeling of wanting to be the most powerful and superior, especially in relationships, and experience being in control. This entails wishing to raise the self-esteem of other people due to the power you have.
- Having covert or criminal agendas. This mostly results in financial manipulation, more so if the victim is defenseless, as in the case of the elderly.
- Lack of identification with underlying feelings; thus having a commitment phobia. A manipulator ends up manipulating unconsciously and convinces themselves on the baselessness of the emotions.

Types of Manipulators

You must have come across the various kinds of manipulators as discussed below, who either manipulated you consciously or unconsciously. So, these are the kinds of people you should learn to avoid before you fall into their traps.

The 'helpless' act: These are the people who brand themselves as helpless to make other people do things that are actually their responsibilities. In many cases, women are the ones who choose these kinds of roles and take advantage of their stereotyped character of 'being weak'. These people are never worried over any type of career so long as they believe they must get people to help them out in case they are stuck.

The skillful-word players: These kinds of manipulators say something in a manner that the victim cannot hold them answerable to their actions. After they see your reactions, they then twist what they had previously mentioned, so it looks like it is you who got them into trouble.

The skillful-word players

Impracticable promises: These kinds of manipulators target you when you are under pressure to get you to make to hasty promises, and then afterward, they guilt you into promising something. Most friends use this mechanism since they think you cannot deny them; after all, you are friends.

Parental manipulation: Many parents are manipulators, though in different cases. Parents impose their own opinions over their children so as to control their children's actions, hence, interfering with their private lives. This makes the children forget about their interests as they live under their parent's control.

Parent-in-law manipulation: Parents, at times, do everything they can to see their children happy, while not understanding that their nagging sometimes contributes to the collapse of happy marriages. Mostly, the mothers tend to impose their views and explanations onto their children on what defines a perfect marriage or a perfect partner.

It is your fault!

The guilty innocent: These manipulators totally disregard the actions and decisions of other people, even their friends, and family members. They regret their behavior and act too fast to blame anyone around them for their own faults. These kinds of manipulators always put it all on you until you feel guilty since they never feel responsible for their own mistakes.

The cost of forgiveness: These kind of a manipulator reveals themselves in your relationships. After disagreements or fights in a relationship, they try to buy their partner's forgiveness through presents and gifts. The gifts or presents act like a bribe as the manipulator uses them to manipulate your gratitude.

The 'It's better for…' kind: This kind of a manipulator deprives you of your right to decide between love and sense of moral duty so as to regulate your actions and life.

Family comes first: These kinds of manipulators are common in families. It is a case where the manipulator tries to convince you having a child is the major point of concern in any relationship. The manipulator tends to point out how significant family ties are in order to manipulate your emotions, to the extent of replacing your own family ties with theirs.

Exaggerated emotions of self-importance: Manipulators are evident in your workplaces. They assign work and give instructions, demonstrating their significance and criticizing the employees. These manipulators always find mistakes in their employees' work and don't tolerate any objections since they yell a lot.

Adult child: Most of the time, these people cannot accept what life offers and end up depending on their parents for everything, even making their parents take care of them as if they are little children. Parents, who are mostly the victims of these kind of manipulators, pay off any debt while their adult kids flow with this life and manipulate their parents.

Influencing People

Influencing and manipulating are close terms that can be easily misinterpreted. Both of them involve creating a particular behavior in a person without having to apply any force necessarily. On the other hand, an influencer is an admirable person whose ways are admired by very many people. Not every kind of influence is always positive: some are negative. In manipulation, the manipulators care about their interests, greed, and they are selfish. Influencing people on the other hand, is grounded upon strong rapport. There is clear communication and a better understanding of those involved.

Neuro-Linguistic Programming (NLP)

Neuro-linguistic programming involves a link between the nervous developments, linguistic and behavior designs acquired through involvement and can be transformed to accomplish particular objectives in natural life. In NLP, you study how well you can communicate with either yourself or with others. It is entirely a method of knowing how well you can achieve your goals or results effectively. When used in manipulation or when influencing people, NLP helps you communicate better with your targets.

Helping people overcome problems at your organization requires having excellent communication skills, and NLP is one of the best techniques to use in either your organization or businesses. Communicating with consumers at their unconscious levels helps them get a better understanding of your products, and this improves your sales.

NLP teaches that you can easily translate what you think into effective verbal communication that can be used in influencing people. You have specific preferences in your thoughts, and you can convert your senses into a strong influence on your targeted prey. The senses; seeing, touching, tasting, smelling, and hearing are your preferred structures that you use to translate whatever is going in your life. Once you get involved with people, you can hear, listen, and you will be able to then tell what their preferred ways of communicating are.

To exploit them, or influence them, you will have to relay back to them specific words or phrases these people often say when you are talking with them. NLP works well with those people you think like you or individuals who have several things in common with you. When communicating, try copying what they do at the moment, and you will notice that your behavior instills some unconscious elements within it.

The chances are these people will like you even more, and it will be easy to influence or manipulate them. If the NLP person is well-conversant with the skills and techniques required, it will be possible to control people without them realizing it.

CHAPTER 1: Practical "xy" technique to influence even a Head of State (used by the secret services)

Along with all the techniques that you have learnt so far, here are a few more, which if you work on committedly will help you achieve the desired results and always achieve success when it comes to manipulating others.

Generate Urgency

To influence, you need to create urgency. Unless you do that, oftentimes, people will not respond as positively as you hope them to. Creating urgency means that you create a scenario or paint a picture of the problem at hand in a manner that it appears as a pressing issue making the other person feel he/she must act as you want. If you want your friend to file for medical insurance, make her feel how urgent that is and how she must not wait another minute to act on it.

Here are some tactics you can use to create urgency in order to manipulate others.

Ask Probing Questions: Asking the right and often probing questions is just the trick that can help you create earnestness in someone to act as desired. If you are tired of your partner not taking his debt issues seriously, ask questions such as 'What problems are we suffering because of financial issues?', 'What are your concerns about your ever-increasing debt?' and 'Is your debt the reason your self-esteem is dwindling?' Make sure to ask the questions with concern in your tone and facial expressions so the other person feels your apprehension and then becomes stimulated to take the desired action.

Give Examples: Another effective tactic to create urgency is to illustrate examples of other people who went through similar experiences, and ended up suffering in the end because they failed to take the right action at the right time. If you wish for your best friend going through depression to get therapy instead of staying engulfed in the darkness all alone, talk to him about how another friend went through the same traumatic episode, but recovered soon after because she had a therapist by her side. Reinforce the urgency by talking about the problem and sharing relevant examples.

Make them Visualize: Visualization is an incredibly effective technique that does not only help you become more invested in your work and put in extra effort to achieve your goals, but also helps you in influencing others as well.

When you wish for someone to oblige to your commands, paint them a beautiful picture of how doing that chore will benefit them. Make them visualize the end outcome and have all their senses involved in the experience so they become fully immersed in the visualization and are then motivated to take the required action.

If you want your students to do well in a certain internship they have signed up for, help them visualize how doing it well will benefit them in the long run and help them land a great job. Make them visualize the sights, sounds, expressions, feelings, sensations and even tastes associated with success. For instance, you can ask them to think of their most favorite ice cream and think of having that when they are successful. Similarly, you can make them think of the sound the ATM makes when your money is about to come out and how you would hear those sounds and feel the touch of crisp dollar bills when you land a fantastic, well paid job.

When you make someone completely involved in an imagination, it targets and influences their subconscious and imbeds relevant suggestions in it. When your subconscious mind becomes focused on a certain outcome, it then makes you work towards achieving that outcome.

Pinpoint the Scarcity: Earnestness can easily be created by using the principle of scarcity. If you want someone to oblige to your demands, let them know how a certain thing is scarce or an offer is only available for a limited time. For instance, if you wish your friend to apply for a scholarship grant for her M.Phil thesis as soon as possible, let her know how the offer ends in 2 days and how she will miss out on a wonderful opportunity by missing it out. If you want your friends to go out on a food festival with you, inform them of how it ends tonight and how all of you will miss a lifetime experience if you do not go today.

While creating urgency, try not to force the other person into doing something. People who are smart enough to realize this tactic are likely to feel offended by it and then distance themselves from you for a while. Thus, do employ the tactics, but very cautiously so people do not feel upset by anything.

Be Aware of Your BATNA

BATNA refers to your 'best alternative to a negotiated agreement' and is your preferred fallback option that you resort to when things do not go, as you want. It is different from the bottom line, which refers to a fixed position that limits the options available to you and keeps you from discovering new actions.

Knowing your BATNA means that you think through a certain situation to come up with different scenarios wherein things do not happen as desired and then opt for a settlement that appeals to you the most. You need to assess the different alternatives available to you and then opt for the most promising substitute that suits you the most.

If, however, you begin negotiation with a bottom line in your demand, you are likely not to explore any other promising options and may have to settle only for it if the negotiations do not go through as planned. Let us share with you an example to explain this better.

If you are trying to get your charity program funded by some big MNC's and are in talks with a few potential sponsors, you need to begin with asking for complete 100% sponsorship that includes every aspect of the event. Your plan B can be to cut it down by 10% or by eliminating one activity from the package instead of asking for only 50% funds as soon as the sponsors reject your initial proposal. If you present different alternatives, it is likely you can get 70% funds and some added benefits instead of just settling for a small amount of funds.

Similarly, if you wish for a colleague to help you out with a project, give him different options instead of withdrawing your request or asking him to do just a little bit if the first initial request of help is unacceptable to him.

Always be aware of your BATNA and present it in an interesting way while offering benefits of doing that to the concerned individual.

Make Use of Objective Criteria

When trying to persuade someone to carry out a certain task, make use of objective criteria. Settle on a framework based on objective criteria using facts, figures, statements and underlying interests, needs, goals and opinions.

For instance, while having an interdepartmental discussion in the company regarding the launch event of a new service, you become quite convinced that you need to rush it to the market as soon as you can. Now if you wish for the entire team to understand that, you need to provide evidence in form of marketing data and tie it in with how all the team members will benefit from incentives and promotions if the launch goes as planned and receives an overwhelmingly positive response as desired.

When choosing objective criteria for a certain matter, take into consideration factors such as market value, legal standards, contractual terms, mission and objectives, vision and other factors according to the nature of the problem.

Be the Authority on the Matter

People like listening and following someone they perceive as an authority figure. If you wish for others to listen to you attentively and dance to your tune, you need to come off as an authority figure on a certain subject matter. If you want someone to take action against physical abuse and end the vicious cycle of codependency she/he is involved in, tell her/him how you have been through the same or dealt with people who underwent that trauma and how putting an end to that pain is crucial for their betterment right now.

To be an authority, you need to have command over the topic and be fully aware of the ins and outs related with it so you have complete knowledge on the issue and can convince others about it easily. If you want your business partner to buy certain software for your small business, become convinced about it first and use your knowledge about it to persuade him then.

Carry out an in depth research on the issue to collect as much data on it as possible and then study it on your own to brush your knowledge of it. It is only when you are well versed on it that you can share it with others, educate others about it and influence them in the desired manner.

Bring in the Element of Empathy

Empathy never goes to waste and always does the trick of winning people over. When being empathetic towards people, remember not to do it just to fulfill your ulterior motives. Empathy is about feeling the pain of others as your own and is something so beautiful that it needs to be incorporated positively in all your actions.

Be your compassionate, loving self with others and be as empathetic as you can with people you genuinely care about. Feel the pain of others, be around them to show your support and do not push anyone to do something he/she feels uncomfortable about. You will build a fantastic rapport with people once you become empathetic towards them and this will only make it easier for you to inspire them.

Remember the Names and Faces of People

An effective way to shower attention on someone especially someone you have only met once or twice is to remember their face and name. People love to build connection with others and when they do, they quickly feel drawn towards that very person. When you meet someone, ask his/her name and use it a couple of times during the conversation so you imbed it in your subconscious mind. Also, pick any prominent facial feature and tie it with that person's name so you remember it easily.

The next time you meet him/her, greet him/her using their name affectionately and it will definitely cheer him/her up drawing them towards you.

Try to make written notes of all the practices you try and how each works out in your favor. Certain tactics work well with certain people while some don't. Therefore, write down about how you implement each tactic so you can keep track of your performance and improve on it the next time.

CHAPTER 2: Achieve your goals thanks to the psychology of persuasion

Two persuasion strategies that are commonly used include the "foot-in-the-entryway," and "entryway in-the-face" methods. In the foot-in-the-entryway procedure, somebody begins with a small and sensible demand—"Do you have sufficient money?"— which at that point leads into a more significant demand—"I need $10 for a taxi."

The entryway in-the-face system is the inverse—it includes somebody making a significant demand, having it rejected, and then retreating to a little demand. Somebody doing contract work, for instance, may approach you for an extensive amount of cash in advance, and then after you refuse, will request a smaller sum. This works since, following the more significant demand, the little request appears to be sensible.

The level of the impact someone has on you is related to control. Envision having the capacity to impact situations when the circumstance calls for it. These two strategies that we discussed are simple enough, yet they can have a large impact on how much we are able to control others and the situations in which we find ourselves with them.

According to a wide body of research, the ability to exert control over other people is easier than you may have thought. One book has had the most significant effect in this field: Robert Cialdini's **Influence**. In it, Cialdini presents the six tools of influence that will enable you to convince others: correspondence, consistency, social verification, liking, authority, and shortage. Throughout the rest of this chapter, we look at these tools of influence and how you can use them to your advantage in order to get what you want.

Tools of Influence

The number one reason individuals will make use of the six tools of influence is to get you to do what they want you to do. We already talked about the common motives that others will have in order to influence you, but let's look at why you might want to use these persuasive tactics on others.

The opportunity to affect individuals often emerges out of obvious needs. Some of them include:

- The need to make changes to a workplace situation

- Authoritative social change

- Tempting more clients to purchase from you

- Urging colleagues to adopt new skills

Acing these six standards of impact will empower you to amplify your capacity for influence. Before we proceed any further, a strong word of caution is needed here. We just spend the first half of this book profiling the despicable ways manipulators feed off other people like parasites. Don't be a manipulator. Do not to mishandle these abilities. There can be a fine line between manipulating others and exerting control. The crucial determiner is motivation. Use these tools the correct way, and you and others will receive benefits.

Humans, as a whole, have the capacity to work in autopilot. Much like a bird sings, a cow produces milk, and hounds bark, we adopt routines and respond in predictable ways, whether learned or instinctive, as though it's our DNA.

We are presented with new information all of the time, yet most of it passes us by. We can't take everything life offers all at once. If we did, we would be overburdened, and our minds couldn't adapt quickly enough. That is where subconscious routines come in.

Our cerebrum deliberately picks a focus to concentrate on and disposes of anything it deems non-essential for the focus. For that reason, numerous activities are performed without conscious thought, and our mental faculties help us lead our daily lives, whereby we respond to new information without knowing about it consciously.

You can utilize these tools and impact strategies to break into people's autopilot programs and lead them to conform to specific conduct. It's important to remember these things:

- Begin in light of the end. Know your targets and what you are seeking to accomplish. What does achievement look like?

- Consider the people whom you are attempting to impact and choose the right impact strategies to suit the circumstance.

- Utilize the procedures to suit.

Correspondence

This is the first tool, and it is often associated with reciprocity. It is the idea that if you do something for a person, they are going to be highly likely to do the same thing for you in return. Part of this is born from obligation and the rules that we use to govern our society. On the other hand, it is also used in order to make them fearful that if they do not return the favor, they won't keep on getting the benefits from you.

Correspondence is a helpful tool to jumpstart a scenario when we need something done. Its supposition is that by acting first and doing something for another person, then you will improve the likelihood of the other party doing what you need accomplished. When we are eager to go first and give before we attempt to get, we have a better shot of engaging others. What useful but unexpected thing would we be able to accomplish for our partners that may acquire us a sympathetic ear when we need to approach them to achieve something for us?

Doing well by others is a shrewd method to get others to do precisely the same thing for you in the future. The only way one could be harmed in this situation is if they aren't reciprocated. It still is never a bad thing to do something nice for someone else. Getting what you want isn't the best reason, but it is sometimes a good enough motivation to help make sure both parties are satisfied.

There are a few different ways to make correspondence work for you. Giving others little blessings, approaching others with deference, and doing favors for those in need are several ways that you can win points with different people.

Consider your goals again and recognize how you can be of assistance to people. It might even be only a vague notion of how you have been of help before. You can start small to see how your efforts are received before risking or committing more. When you perceive that your gifts or favor have been received positively, then you can either wait to allow reciprocation, or you can offer another kindness. But it's important to keep a delicate balance in the relationship. The principle is about correspondence. If you go too far in giving without the other party having opportunity to give back, you can cause discomfort or alienation.

Conventional methodology is to help other people and be benevolent when you have the chance since no one can tell how it might enable you to down the line. Besides, it is these little demonstrations of thoughtfulness that will be recollected and prove to be useful when you need some help in the near future.

Consider when you got a present or a birthday card from somebody you are not typically used to accepting one from. What sway did that have on you? How did that affect your thoughts? Did it cause you to take any specific action? You may have sent them a birthday card or present back. For what reason is this? It is mostly because of the principal weapon of impact: the standard of response. This standard state that we should attempt to reimburse, in kind, what someone else has provided to us.

For instance, if a friend sends us a birthday present, we ought to recognize his birthday with our very own gift; if two or three welcome us to a gathering, we ought to make sure to welcome them to one of our own. By keeping the correspondence rule, we are committed to the future reimbursement of favors, blessings, solicitations, and so forth.

For what reason do we do this? It is straightforward; we feel committed to respond in kind because of a sentiment of obligation. Furthermore, it is our ingrained culture and conviction frameworks that constrain us into compensating such debt.

Ensure that you aren't doing kind things for others simply to get something from a person. We still should be considerate of others, giving and thoughtful in all aspects of life. If you only do things because you are expecting something back from the other person, then this can lead to a lot of disappointment, and it can also become a form of manipulation. There can be a subtle difference between giving and buying.

Yet correspondence is a rule of thumb we need to have in all of our relationships, both romantic and as friends. How could we expect respect, love, and understanding from other individuals if we aren't willing to give them the same? It has been said that the best marriage is not one where each side gives 50%, but where each partner gives 100%. That is the principle of correspondence.

This sort of "bribery" can still be very powerful when used correctly. If you are going to ask for something from your boss, then you would want to wait until the end of the day and perform your best abilities in order to somewhat "butter them up." If you are wanting to ask your parents or partner for some money to buy something you want, you might make them dinner first. These are ways of finding the "opportune moment" that provides the best conditions for you to achieve the result you desire. It is shrewd, but not necessarily manipulative.

The important distinction between using this for influence and not manipulation is to ensure that you aren't expecting them to do something that is going to hurt them. That could then be considered threatening or in some situations, blackmailing. Instead, only have good intentions and make sure you are never influencing a person to do things that would make them uncomfortable.

Consistency

One of the main reasons behind manipulation is the quest for self-devised expectations. Manipulators take drastic actions because of their fears or insecurities that they will not get what they think they need. You can help all of the people around you—not just those who are manipulative—by ensuring consistency in what you do. When you become a dependable and reliable person, it will automatically make you even more influential.

When you stick to your word or do what you say, then people know that they can rely on you to get the outcome that they are envisioning. Once you have established such trustworthiness, it becomes much easier to influence the actions of others. They will trust you, so when you offer advice and start to guide them in a particular direction, it will be much easier for them to listen to your words.

There are three aspects to consistency: responsibility, sincerity, and intentionality. The first aspect is a functioning responsibility. By this, Cialdini means that an individual must make a specific choice to accept responsibility for whatever issue is at hand. If you are not willing to commit fully and in a personal way, but create a contingency plan if things go bag or ensure that there is an escape route, then you have not embraced responsibility and it's up to mere chance whether you will succeed. Certainly, you will not develop influence with others because of the quality of consistency.

Once you have made a personal commitment to be responsible for an issue or concern, you need to make your commitment public. Stating to others that you will accomplish a particular task is a great start to getting it done. It demonstrates your sincerity about the task at hand. Your public declaration of your responsibility demonstrates that you are willing to risk your reputation for the outcome. Then when you know that other people are watching, there is a simple accountability of others knowing that you are responsible which makes you more prone to finish.

Third, you need to follow through on what you have committed to yourself and to others. You must intentionally work toward the outcome. The beauty of this aspect of consistency is that even if you do not succeed in the ways that you and others expected, when you exert focused effort to bring about the outcome you've envisioned, you will still earn the credibility associated with consistency. The payoff may not be as great as if you did exactly as hoped, or even better, but you will earn points for trying.

Think about this: when you've put down a wager on a bet or purchased a lottery ticket, have you at any point felt more confident that you are going to win than you did just before acting on that risk? Did your perspective shift from vulnerability to conviction? Professional athletes have long used the technique of visualization, repeatedly imagining themselves accomplishing their desired outcomes, to promote their success on the field, and the principle is similar. When a person has confidence, optimism, and the drive to achieve an outcome, the likelihood of success increases.

Our brains are highly adaptable, but we may also consider them lazy. That is, when there is a predetermined course of action, it becomes the default course for our brains. This reality originates from our innate preference for steadiness and predictability around us. The principle of consistency leverages this tendency. Rather than expending energy to strike off in a new direction, we are much more likely to expend energy on something for which we already feel responsible. When a person settles on a decision, his brain will align to the completion of that course of action. He reacts in manners that legitimize his prior choice. Even in the face of difficulty, he persuades himself that he has settled on the correct decision and will persevere in it. To do otherwise causes stress and cognitive dissonance.

Have a look at the following example: An experiment in New York was conducted to detect human behavior in certain circumstances. For this experiment, an ordinary radio was left on a towel near a large group of beachgoers. A staged snatch-and-grab was conducted to see how people would react.

For the first part of the experiment, when the staged robbery occurred, only four out of twenty individuals responded to the theft. For the second part of the research, a selected individual asked certain bystanders to watch his radio while he attended to a matter elsewhere.

In this second scenario, it was found that nineteen out of twenty people became vigilant toward their surroundings and reacted when the staged robbery occurred. Here we see the illustration of consistency in real life.

This sort of thinking is so ingrained in us that it produces a bias for how we view people. Almost universally, individuals who are steady, rational, and responsible in everyday life situations are regarded with respect, trust, and admiration.

Consistency shows up regularly in our casual social situations, as well. We often, as a kind gesture, ask individuals how they are doing. Whether they are doing fine or not, you expect them to tell you everything is fine. Through consistency, we tend to accept the general idea of something without honestly thinking or reacting to it.

It is common for someone to ask a friend, "If I do this, would you do it too?" Whether the thing in question is safe or not, individuals will be more comfortable doing something just because another person, with whom they have a connection or sense of responsibility, is doing it. The principle of consistency therefore helps explain the power of peer pressure.

So how would you utilize this reality of consistency as a tool? When you demonstrate the character of a consistent and reliable person, then others will be more apt to trust you and to look to you for important details. And by going on record as responsible, you make your success more likely.

Likewise, you improve your chances of influencing another person and leading them to your desired destination if you can get them to embrace even the smallest form of responsibility and to do so in a public or interpersonal way. In a sales environment, surveys or product testing are great ways to do this, especially in the context of improving the product's performance or safety for others' benefit. Your subject then becomes an ally, helping you to reach your goal of having a better product. Their personal investment can then become a means for them to develop a desire for the product or service you are offering.

In a setting in which you must lead a meeting, you can create buy-in before you even enter the boardroom by giving your peers a small but engaging task or issue to consider as preparation. If done well, this will build enthusiasm and create a foundation for them to publicly commit to investing as you desire in your project. Be sure to find ways to validate and incorporate whatever each person prepared in order to give them a sense of contribution.

In a coaching or a mentoring role, you should encourage your student to embrace responsibility **in the right situations** and then follow these aspects of the consistency tool. She should inform others of her commitment, and then work diligently to make it happen. As you guide her, you can help her to understand the great value of these deposits toward establishing her character and reputation amongst others—and conversely, the harm and lasting damage that can occur from being inconsistent. Such inconsistency can take the form of both disengagements, an unwillingness to commit to be responsible, and negligence, not successfully following through when a commitment has been made.

<u>Social Verification</u>

We've all heard the saying, "If so-and-so jumped off a bridge, would you do it too?" There are some instances where we might even say, "Yes!" because we are so trusting of that person. This is essentially what social verification is. When you can show that others are thinking the same way, they have the same faith in an idea, and that there is social proof to validate the proposition, then it will be easier to have influence over others.

Frequently, individuals depend on meaningful gestures from others to guide how they think, feel, and act. Not everyone is a legitimate source for this kind of guidance; we tend to lend more credibility to others who are most similar to us.

You've probably heard about or seen in action the idea of a "plant" in a crowd, who is designed to jumpstart a particular desired response to an opportunity. Once that individual proclaims a desire to buy a magic tomato slicer, then somebody else who really did want one but was shy has the courage to call out. And the force of multiple voices accumulates, convincing others who are undecided. In its ugliest form, we see the principle of social verification take place in the "mob mentality," when a crowd forms to do harm with little regard for the consequences. Individual standards become blurred in favor of the mob's rampant energy and intensity.

In a more personal setting, the principle of social verification is used all of the time to rally support for an idea or initiative. When initiating change, it is a common strategy to individually seek out influential people within the community or workspace, attempting to win them over to the strategy, and asking them to support the effort by speaking well of it to others. When the others see a representative, who is similar to themselves offering support, they are more likely to follow in the same way. Having that first individual make a move has a significant effect and activates the tool of social verification.

Think about the last time you shopped for something on the web, perhaps a book from Amazon or a vacation rental on the beach through TripAdvisor. What did you do before you chose to purchase? You looked at the surveys, right?

The answer may seem obvious, but why did you do that? You suppose that if it is sufficient for countless others, then it must be at least adequate for you. And after all, five stars are five stars! But it's a fairly high level of trust that we place in the opinions of other people—people whom we have never met before and about whom we know very little. Yet we make major decisions that impact our personal lives, our families, our finances, and our careers, based on the pithy reviews offered by anonymous individuals on the internet (where you can trust everything, right?). This is a pretty astounding example of the power of social verification to guide and influence our behaviors and decisions. It reveals that one method we use to figure out what is right is to discover what other individuals believe is right.

The rule of social verification is also powerful because it can apply particularly to the manner in which we choose what establishes right conduct. We often see behavior as increasingly correct to the extent that we see others performing it. So, when we are in a condition of vulnerability or uncertainty, it is human instinct for us to look to people around us for direction on which move to make.

There are a number of ways you can use social verification to your advantage, especially as a business person or someone in charge of advertising. One powerful method is to tap into internet-based life stages. Consider when you are searching for an item or finding out about something new. Both our initial investigations and our ultimate decisions can be heavily influenced by the number of fans, endorsements, and supporters. Pages or profiles with a large number of devotees are viewed as experts in their specialty and usually grow more and receive special consideration because of their reach and broad influence. Exploit these life stages and communities with focused promotion.

Reviews, testimonials, and compliments are another incredible asset for using the tool of social verification, especially in a web-based setting. It is a basic rule of marketing that you accumulate surveys and comments from your happy clients and utilize those to assemble trust with new clients. Statements from the horse's mouth are the most effective.

To be sure, the principle of social verification is usually at its most influential in situations where someone seeks a resolution or an answer to a question. Think, for instance, of someone traveling internationally for the first time. As she encounters strange cultural phenomena and cannot understand what is written or the things people say, she glances around. She watches what other people are doing, and she follows suit. Sometimes it ends up in embarrassment, most of the time, it's the path to success.

Yet social verification can also accomplish results even when people have what they deem a perfectly good, predetermined behavior and have no question in their mind. Cialdini and a research group directed a test to perceive what kind of information on signs would result in inn visitors reusing their washroom towels.

- Sign 1 referred to ecological reasons.

- Sign 2 said the inn would give a donation to an ecological cause.

- Sign 3 said the inn had already made a donation and asked: "Will you please go along with us?"

- Sign 4 said most inn visitors reused their towels once while staying at the inn.

At the point when visitors were informed that most other lodging visitors were reusing their towels, they were bound to agree to the solicitation. Sign #4 got 48 percent of participants to reuse their towels.

Liking

Offering compliments, sharing praise, and generally being a friend to someone is enough to persuade them on some levels. This is why social media has so much influence. When we can strive for "likes" from other people and get those likes, we are reassured in our decisions. It is the validation needed in order to influence us to keep going.

People like the individuals who like them or whom they see as companions. It is a basic, yet powerful thought. The tool of preference can be utilized in a couple of ways.

One strategy is discovering shared values with anyone you meet. If you can connect with them on their pastimes or interests, you'll have a firm ground to work from. All this requires is asking good questions and listening well.

Another method of building affinity with others is offering encouragement and sincere compliments.

Especially when the things you notice and affirm in others provides them with keen insight into themselves, you can play an important role of influencing them to grow and build their areas of strength. The key here is real commendation and not flattery. Insincere or embellished praise can come off as creepy and can easily do just as much harm as sincere compliments provide benefits.

Give real commendation and positive criticism to your colleagues. Begin by observing yourself and noting how frequently you offer positive versus negative criticism in a day. Like the majority of us, you might be astonished! Strive to offer positive compliments three times as often as you do negative ones.

To be a good friend, focus more on giving than on receiving. As you relate to others, be consistent and reasonable with the things that you are asking of them. If you aren't willing to do it yourself, why should someone else do it for you? Let individuals know you are there for them when they need you. Be transparent; act naturally, and don't make a special effort to be popular or winsome. Merely treat others how you would like to be treated, and most reasonable people will be happy in your presence. These are important elements in building trust.

Have you ever driven twice as far to make a simple grocery purchase just because you like the staff of one establishment better than the shops closer to you? Whether or not you feel comfortable in a place and enjoy the experience while you are there can be as important a consideration as price or selection of products.

Consider salespeople. The most important thing a sales rep will do is get a sense of who you are and what you need first. Only then will he or she proceed to offer you products or services that may help your specific needs and wants. Oftentimes, we can see a salesperson's maneuvers a mile away, as he obviously tries to find an area of common ground. The best salespeople have a knack for cracking through resistance, though, and finding a way to make a connection with a customer, even when his efforts to be likable are obvious.

To use the tool of liking, keep in mind that you will probably sabotage your efforts if you try too hard and scheme too much. When the tool works its best, you are able to make use of a natural point of commonality with another person. You shouldn't fabricate information about yourself to establish such connections. But you recognize a point in common with another person, you can artfully accentuate that point and build the relationship around it. An exchange about a most loved game or sports crew is an extraordinary case of this. It is only human to be more engaging or like someone more if they show interest in us or compliment us on something. With that said, we are more prone to agree about or purchase something from someone based on them liking us.

This tool is also helpful in large group settings. If you have the occasion to speak before a crowd, you should think in advance about the best way to present yourself. What should you wear? Are there any changes you should make to the way you speak? What stories can you tell that will especially resonate with the group? You don't want to be a sell-out, but if there is a version of yourself that fits best in that crowd, then employ that person to create the highest level of affinity. Ultimately, if you use this tool correctly, you will provide benefits for yourself and the people who like you.

Authority

Authority figures can have some of the greatest influence. If you are driving and there is a cop behind you, that influences you to go the speed limit, simply because of their presence. When you are taking a test, the authority figures at the front of the room are influencing you to not cheat and look at the papers of other students. This may be the easiest tool to create influence, but it is also the most misused.

If you are going about being authoritative in the wrong way, not only will others fail to listen to you, but they might end up being actively insubordinate. Parents who are too hard on their kids can end up driving them away, and that teen might rebel simply for the sake of angering their parents. It is important to find the line between too strict and too permissive when using this tool of persuasion.

We tend to think of authority in terms of someone with a commanding personality or a high-level position barking out commands and orders to underlings. To be sure, that image is one aspect of authority. But there is another way to be an authority in a way that is more subtle and perhaps more influential in the long run. When you are seen as a specialist or expert in a field, your knowledge or expertise establishes you as an authority, and others will seek you because they desire the potential you offer to impact their growth. People trust those who know what they are talking about and are confident in what they are about to do since they have done it many times before.

Other people will have less noble aspirations and may simply seek to take advantage of your prestige or network. For this reason, thought leaders and those with notoriety have to be discerning. Unlike the other tools for persuasion that we have discussed, this is one where other people will seek you out more than you have to try and exert influence on others. You then run the risk of finding yourself manipulated.

Most of us have some area of skill or knowledge that can benefit others yet without widespread appeal. In this case, what you have to offer may travel by word of mouth over a prolonged period of time. True, in a workplace environment, you can send your resume out to your entire team on your first day in the office and display certificates and plaques on the walls of your workspace. But such behaviors reek of pride and turn away the most teachable individuals, who would be likely to put to good use any knowledge you share.

Another strategy to make your abilities known in a less demonstrative way is to pepper your conversations with little bits and pieces of information related to your interests and expertise. If people are listening well and have an interest in the same area, they will eventually ask for more information. This casual means of sharing your ability places you in the best possible position to use your authority in a persuasive and influential way.

Become an expert and do what you love doing most. The more you know and do correctly, the more influential your authority will be. And don't be deceived into thinking that influence has just fallen into the laps of the most successful people you see in the public eye. Most of them have worked tirelessly and relentlessly to be better at their area than anyone else. Work hard, and you will have great experience from which to guide others.

Shortage

"While supplies last," "limited edition," "exclusive," and other terms like this are often used as marketing strategies to get people more interested. Dunkin Donuts might come out with a new product and say it is limited edition as if it were some rare flavor of coffee never to be replicated again. In reality, the actual ingredient might not differ much from something they already have, and they are simply using this tactic to get more people interested in the product.

Shortage and scarcity can be very helpful when you are attempting to influence others. Making them feel as though they have a rare opportunity will make them more likely to jump on the offer, pressuring them and giving them the sense that they have to act now, or they will find out they are too late to enjoy something fantastic.

Individuals appreciate what is rare, and value usually increases when scarcity increases. Just think about how you would feel if you urgently need an item and scurry to purchase it only to find out it is no longer in stock?

Consider a shortage of fuel, a highly practical and therefore valuable commodity in our society. A mass lack of fuel—and it has happened in the past—means prices skyrocketing, long lines for even a gallon of fuel, and emergency protocols for businesses, agencies, and citizens as new methods of getting simple things done would need to be established.

The more rare something is, the more prominent the urge to acquire it. A dread of not having something can stir individuals into a free-for-all, making them frantic not to pass up a great opportunity. Ironically, the impulse to avoid missing out on something is stronger than the urge to have something. So this is a tool that comes with a great deal of potential.

Lines for the most recent iPhone, computer game, show tickets, and the franticness of the shopping extravaganza following Thanksgiving are further examples of the lengths to which individuals will go when the weapon of shortage comes into play.

There are a couple of ways that you can utilize the standard of shortage to induce others. These include making offers constrained to time, restricting supply, or providing one-time offers, all of which create feelings of deficiency.

One way that scarcity plays on our human psychology is that we have a natural bias toward believing that something that is rare or scarce is better. Perhaps the idea is influenced somewhat by the idea of social verification—if so many people wanted something that there is little left, then it must be outstanding. Scenarios in which there appears to be a selection process play on human pride and appeal to the ego. This is why people pay exorbitant fees to be members of exclusive country clubs and elite societies. There is a feeling of status and importance that comes from such associations.

If you are selling an item, customers will be moved to respond more urgently when given a time limit or when warned that supplies are limited. Yet those factors alone will not complete the persuasive element of scarcity. You must also help potential customers envision the consequences if they do not act quickly.

Similarly, the tactic of shortage can be used as a simple means of leading people to make a decision. Simply, they must assess whether their lives will be better with an item or without an item, in a condition of shortage. If you can help them imagine these scenarios, ideally with the acquisition as positive and the shortage as negative, then you will help them to make their decision. Of course, you don't want to be dishonest, and you must not confuse your motivation for profit with the motivation to bring about good in the life of another. Otherwise, you will twist this influential skill into manipulation.

The tool of shortage can help in a sales setting or when making business pitches, but you don't want to always use it on a personal level. For example, you might want to tell your friends you can't hang out that often, even though your schedule is free, just so they will be more likely to reach out to you. This would be considered manipulation.

Just because using shortage in our personal lives in unethical doesn't mean there won't be people who try to use it. Think of those individuals who seem to have a lot of friends, but not many that they are close with. This "popular" status has allowed them to consistently have admiration from others. One of the reasons that they might be able to achieve this status is because of scarcity.

Maybe they always show up late to a party and leave before others as well. Perhaps they rarely text back, making you feel desperate for answer when you do the texting first. They might withhold emotion so that when they are compassionate, this feels like a special and rare treat.

You might consider this in your personal life, but always be aware of who is on the other side. A better way to implement this strategy would be to do so through social media, or if you were trying to build your brand and gain popularity in that sense.

Posting less often means that when you do post a picture on social media, for example, people will be more excited and likely to click "like" than they would for a person who posts three times a day. Others will be more excited for new content if you wait to strategically release it rather than if you are constantly giving things away for free.

Some individuals like a challenge or like to feel like they are working for something, so they will be more likely to try harder to win you over to get your approval when you are scarce rather than overly giving.

This would be most simply seen by a woman waiting until the fifth or sixth date to engage in romantic activities in order to make their partner more interested. Be cautious as this strategy doesn't always work. There will be some individuals who become simply bored with waiting around, and they won't always be as willing to pay out higher costs for things that seem "rare" or "exclusive."

CHAPTER 3: Mindset 3%: understand the mental patterns of 3% of the world population and reach success too!

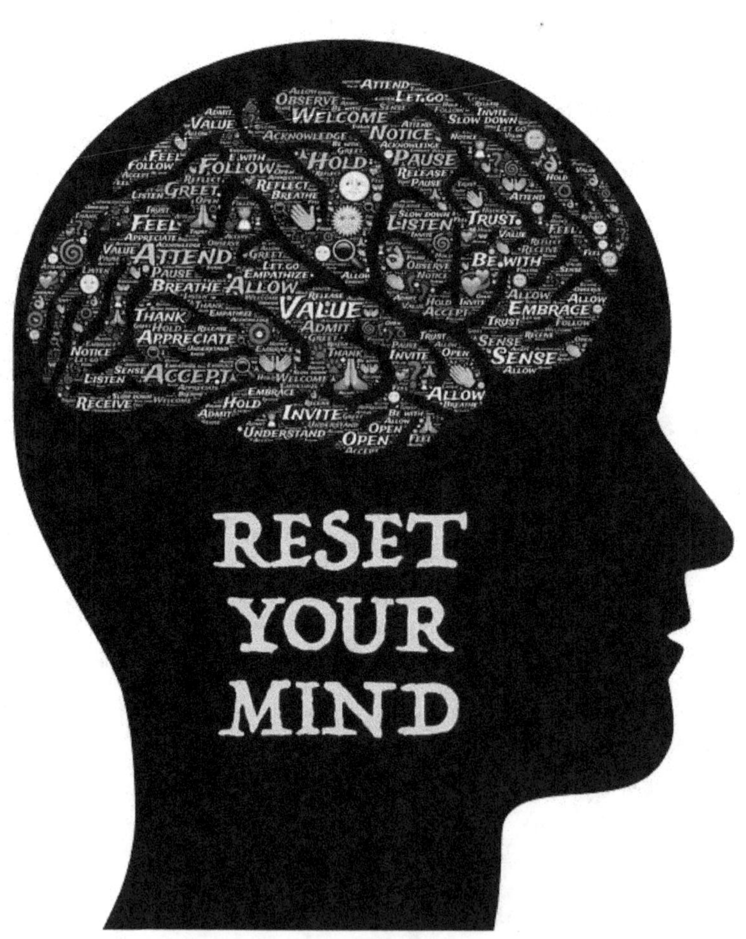

The power of persuasion means nothing more than using mental abilities to form words and feelings used to convince other people to do things they may or may not want to do. Some people are better able to persuade than other people. And some people are easier to persuade then other people.

The ease of persuading other people is directly tied to their current mental or emotional state. Someone who is lonely or tired is easier to persuade, simply because their defenses are lowered. Someone who is momentarily needy may be easier to persuade than someone who has a strong sense of self-worth. People who are at a low point in their lives are easy prey for others who might try to persuade them to do something they might not usually do.

Think of the publicity surrounding religious cults in the past. Everyone wanted to know how someone could fall prey to the teachings and ideals of the cult. The answer is simple: the victim was seeking something the cult offered. Whether the dangling carrot was food and shelter or love or religious freedom, the cult offers something tangible to the person who feels their life is lacking something important. And the person who joins the cult does not see themselves as a victim, but a participant. Think back further to the flower children of the sixties and seventies. These people lived in communes where everyone had a particular role to play. Some people would grow gardens to feed the members of the commune while others might wash laundry or clean houses. Everyone helped everyone else. The idea behind living in a commune was to leave behind the trappings that 'society' deemed as markers of success, such as fat paychecks and huge houses. These people wanted to live simply and enjoy what love and Mother Nature had to offer.

For every good group that assembles for the good of the people and works to help its members, there are countless groups that are brought together by forces that have no desire other than controlling other people for their own good. These leaders are very charismatic and very dangerous, because a person who is temporarily weak in mind or in the soul may not be able to resist their promises. It is important for everyone to understand how persuasion works in order to be able to resist it when needed.

The first step in persuasion involves the idea of reciprocating. If a person does something nice for someone else, then the receiving person usually feels the need to do something good in return. If someone helps their elderly neighbor carry in groceries from the car, that neighbor might feel obligated to bake homemade cookies for that person. A coworker who helps complete a project is more likely to receive assistance when it is needed. Many people do nice things for others all the time without expecting anything in return. The person who does nice things for people and then mentions some little favor that can be done in return may be someone to watch closely.

Nonprofit organizations use this tactic to gain more contributions to their causes. They will often send some little trinket or gift to prompt people to donate larger sums of money, or even just to donate where they might not have originally. The idea behind this is that the person opening the letter has received a little gift for no reason, so they might feel obligated to give something in return.

The consistency of self is the next step. People who commit to something, through verbal or written methods, are more likely to follow through on the idea that someone who makes no promises, Even if the original motivation is gone or the original incentive was taken away, people see this promise as being part of their image. They made a promise. This is often why counselors tell people to write their goals down. People are more likely to follow a written list they can refer to daily.

It is easy enough to change someone's image of themselves, especially if that person is needy or mentally weak. During times of war, it is customary to get prisoners to denounce their own country in order to hopefully turn others against that country. This is easy enough to do when starved prisoners are also mentally weak and have few defenses to use to deflect their captors. By constantly repeating statements that denounce the home country the captive begins to believe what they are saying because it must be true because they are saying it.

Another thing to be careful of is what is known as the herd mentality. Humans live in groups. Most of us want to belong to the herd and want to enjoy the safety being in a herd brings. Monkey see, monkey do. People tend to mirror the behavior seen around them. Think of the story of the emperor that runs around with no clothes on. His tailors had him convinced he was wearing fine garments, so he convinced all the people of his kingdom. And because they could not question the king, they had to believe what he was saying. This can also work in seriously negative ways. Think of the mob mentality. This is just another way to follow the herd, but it usually involves illegal or dangerous activities engaged in only because someone else was doing the same thing.

Some people are automatically tempted to follow authority. People in positions of authority can command blind respect to their authority simply by acting a certain way or putting on a uniform. The problem with this is that authority figures or those that look like authority figures, can cause some people to do extraordinary things they would not normally do had a person in a position of authority not been the one asking. And it is not simply held to people in uniform. People who carry themselves a certain way or speak a certain way can give the impression that they are something they are not.

For someone or something to be considered a credible authority, it must be familiar and people must have trust in the person or organization. Someone who knows all there is to know about a subject is considered an expert and is more likely to be trusted than someone who has limited knowledge of the subject. But the information must also make sense to the people hearing it. If there is not some semblance of accuracy and intelligence then the authority figure loses credibility. Even the person who is acknowledged as an expert will lack persuasive abilities if they are seen as not being trustworthy.

People want to be liked. People want to like other people. The problem is when some people use this fact to cause other people to do things they might not ordinarily do. People who are easy to like usually come across as very persuasive. People want to believe them. Con artists are extremely likeable people. The problem is that even likeable people may not have your personal best interests at heart. In fact, they probably only have their own interest in mind. Even someone who is totally legitimate, like a salesperson, is really most interested in their own interests. They may want their customer to be perfectly happy with their purchase so they will recommend that salesperson to their friends, but their ultimate concern is with themselves and their sales goals.

The worst part of the power that goes along with persuasion is that things that are scarce or hard to get are seen as much more valuable. People value diamonds because they are expensive and beautiful. If they were merely pretty stones, they would not be as interesting. Inconsistent rewards are a lot more interesting than consistent rewards. If a cookie falls every time a person rings a bell, then they are less likely to spend a lot of time ringing the bell because they know the cookie reward will always appear. If, however, the cookie only appears sometimes, people will spend much more time ringing the bell just in case this is the time the cookie will fall.

There are ways to improve the power of persuasion. Just like any other trait, it can be made stronger by following a few strategies and by regular practice.

Never hesitate to ask others what they think. Usually, those in a position of authority will not look for advice from other people. This is an opportunity many leaders neglect to take advantage of. Instead of asking others for their opinion and ideas, they miss the chance to make everyone feel like part of the group with an equal role to play. Besides, leaders who are not afraid to ask for input from others might learn something they did not know before.

Always remember to ask for advice, not feedback. People love being asked to give advice. Asking for feedback means that an opinion has already been given and the speaker wants to know what everyone else thinks of their own opinion. In many situations, there will be no responses because no one wants to disagree or be seen as argumentative, particularly with an authority figure. But asking for advice gives people a chance to voice their own opinions.

Before asking for any type of assistance, set the stage. People do not like being put on the spot. Walking up to someone and immediately asking for a favor sends two messages. The first one is that the favor is more important than the person. In this case, the favor needed is the focus of the conversation. Say that Bob walks into the room, goes straight up to Bill and asks Bill to assist at a fundraiser that weekend. Bill is caught off guard and must make an immediate decision. Does he say no, in front of others, and look like a mean-spirited person for not helping at the fundraiser? Or does he answer with yes without really knowing if he wants to do it or not? Whichever way the conversation goes, when Bill looks back on it later he may wonder if Bill even considers him a friend or if he just comes around when he wants help with something.

Now if Bob had bothered to set the stage for asking for the favor, he would have approached the conversation in a totally different manner. First, he would have approached Bill with a friendly greeting and cheerful smile. He would take a few minutes to make small talk with Bill, perhaps asking about his work life or his family life. After chatting cheerfully for a few minutes Bob would approach the idea of the fundraiser in a casual manner. "Hey, Bill, by the way…." He would explain what he needed Bill to do, explain how much he would really enjoy having Bill's presence at the fundraiser, then asking Bill to get back with him as soon as possible with an answer. He would assure Bill that whatever decision he made would be fine, although he really hoped Bill would be able to join him.

What is the difference between the two situations? In the second situation, Bill feels wanted. He feels needed. He feels as though his presence, or the lack of it, is important to Bob. In the second situation, Bob is most likely to get an honest answer. And what if Bill is not able to help Bob at the fundraiser? Bill will be more likely to help Bob in the future because he not only feels valued but he feels like he owes Bob something,

Bill would probably be thinking that he owed Bob one in the future.

Persuasion is a powerful tool in the game of life. Persuasive people know that they have an amazing power, and they know how to use it correctly. They know how to listen and really hear what other people have to say. They are very good at making a connection with other people, and this makes them seem even more honest and friendly. They make others feel that they are knowledgeable and can offer a certain sense of satisfaction. They also know when to momentarily retreat and regroup. They are not pushy. They are persuasive.

CHAPTER 4: Technique of fear: use it to make anyone do what you want

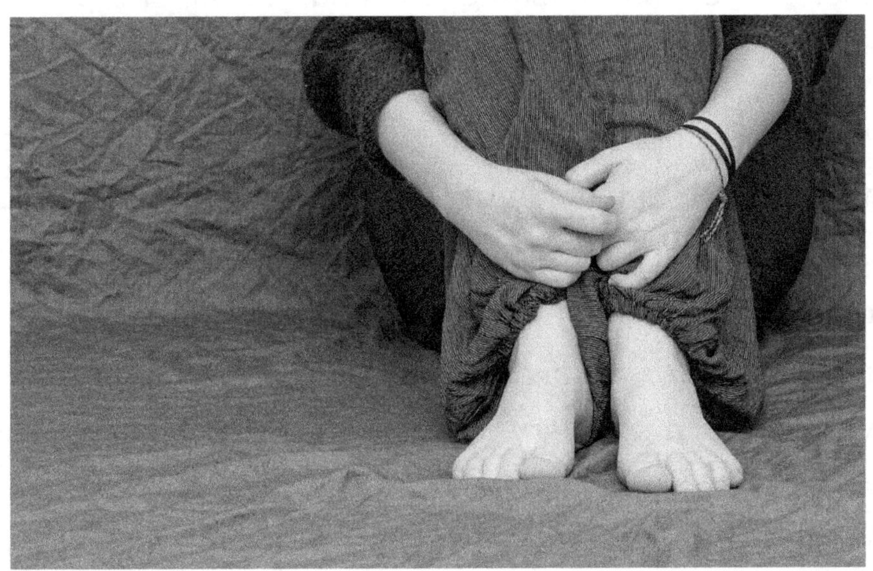

Emotional manipulation is the systematic control over one person by another using the victim's emotions against them. It is emotional abuse where one party takes advantage of the other regardless of the damage it may do to them. It can come in many forms. It may be subtle like a gesture or a disapproving look. Or it can be loud outbursts or even violent. Whatever form it takes, the aim is the same: to bend the will of a person and control them.

All manipulators use specific tools and tactics, whatever the form of manipulation they practice. Money is a tool used to manipulate people into doing things they otherwise would not do. People are routinely twisted into knots by manipulators using power and sex. Everywhere and every day, we are manipulated by people who have the things we want or need. This is just life. If you want something, there is a price. If you choose to chase power, the tradeoff is that you have to do things you don't want to do. Things like doing extra hours at work or spending time with people you don't like. This is good old-fashioned honest manipulation.

Emotional or psychological manipulation is much different. The tool emotional manipulators employ is **you,** or more accurately, perceived weaknesses in your character. They analyze your personality and identify weak spots which they use against you. Far from being honest, they are deceptive to the point that you may not even realize it's happening to you. They bend your thinking and how you see the world so that they can control your behavior. Because the emotions that spur you to act are your own, you don't realize that you have been pushed to do something you don't want to do. You think that you make the decisions to do things that you don't want to do. You go through the torment, but you don't get the benefit. The person manipulating you gets all the reward for your suffering.

People use emotional manipulation for many reasons. It can be used to get things from you like money, sex, or often a place to live and a caretaker. They do it because they feel entitled to a better life and taking from you or someone else is how they accomplish it. There are no concern effects on you beyond what makes you easier to control. Whether it is, a parent who wants to spend more time with you, the unemployed boyfriend/ girlfriend staying at your house, or the co-worker who wants you to do their work for them; they feel entitled to take from you. They have no qualms about treating you like a child, manipulating you to do what they want you to do.

Speaking of treating you like a child, why isn't parenting considered emotional manipulation? Parenting can be seen as positively influencing kids. Many of the same tactics used in raising children are emotional manipulation. It's mostly the same thing. In fact, it can be argued that it is the exact same thing with one exception: intent. When raising a child, your intent is benevolent. You want only the best for them and you "influence" them for their benefit.

When you are controlling someone and profiting from the damage you are doing to them, it is abuse. Parenting only becomes manipulation if the parent is benefiting and the child is harmed. Arguably some parents of beauty pageant kids or child actors cross the line between beneficial and parasitical, but most parents are not manipulating their children.

Manipulation is a parasitical relationship in which one party benefits and one party suffers. When confronted, a manipulator may say he/she was only doing what was best for you. This is how they try to blur the line between what is harmful and what is beneficial to you. You are the one who gets to decide if you are being harmed or not. It is your life, and you know if you have been taken from. They may say they do it for you, but they are helping themselves to what rightly belongs to you. They are harming you and being rewarded for doing it. They are manipulating you.

Recognizing manipulation

Emotional manipulators, in order to be effective, must hide their motives and tactics from you. If they can't successfully cloak their intentions, they can't successfully trick you into changing behavior. They learn to be very effective in discerning openings into people's defenses and hiding the fact that they are doing it. Because they have spent their lifetime training in deception, they are generally highly skilled at it. It is understandable that most people who are being manipulated don't even know it.

So, how do you determine if you are being manipulated or not? There are signs/symptoms of emotional manipulation. They can be indicators that you are being manipulated, but there are also ingrained aspects of our personalities that can make us susceptible to being manipulated. The two things are not mutually exclusive. If you are generally a fearful person, the manipulator will use fear to control you. Fear is then both a predisposing factor and a symptom of abuse. These fear and shame feedback loops are very beneficial to the manipulator. They require little effort to kindle because they are self-perpetuating. The abuser wants to build on a weakness that is already evident in you. It makes their work easier. The traits that can be used to exploit you are probably the characteristics that drew them to you in the first place.

Personality traits that can make you susceptible to emotional manipulation

Too trusting - Some people are naturally trusting of others. They will allow people they do not know the opportunity to hurt them.

Indistinct boundaries - A person who wants to control you will test your boundaries. If you don't have any or they are intermittent, you will be taken advantage of.

History of abuse - Growing up with a parent or other manipulative relative can make it seem normal or even comfortable to be around. You may be the perfect target for manipulators because you've already been conditioned to abusive behavior.

Self-doubt - This is both a contributing factor as well as a symptom of emotional manipulation. One of the goals of the abuser is to make you doubt reality as well as your abilities and value as a human being so that you can be more easily controlled. If you are a person filled with self-doubt, to begin with, it is much easier for the abuser to get from you what they want. The effects of being manipulated are subtle. Usually, they are instilled in you over long periods of time, so changes are harder to spot. Also, they tend to dovetail into your pre-existing emotional pallet. They almost always feed on themselves and get amplified. Low self-esteem allows you to be controlled by someone who lowers your self-esteem further, making controlling you easier. It can be a cycle that is advantageous to the manipulator. Emotional manipulation can manifest itself as increased levels of toxic emotions, which further ensnare you into an abusers web. Examples of these symptoms are as follows:

Shame - You often feels ashamed of you. It can be about how you look or some episode from your past. You dwell on it and are convinced you are undeserving because of it. Shame is used by abusers to break down your barriers so you will allow them to do things to you that otherwise, you would not allow.

Guilt - The same as shame, except that with guilt, comes the feeling that a debt is owed. Emotional manipulators will bring up past transgressions and hold them over you in order to get what they want. The guiltier you feel, the more they can get from you in penance.

Fear - You fears a person or their reactions with you in some way. It might be fear of physical violence, or fear that you have done something wrong and will get in trouble for it. You may fear what a person's mood will be like when you see them.

Low self-esteem - You feel unworthy of being loved, liked, or even accepted. There is usually a laundry list of reasons you carry with you to support your low self-esteem. Manipulators try to keep you in this state so that you are more likely to take the abuse they give you.

Losing your sense of what is real - You feel like your sanity is slipping away. You are unsure what is true and what is a lie. You have contradictory information swimming around your head and can't make decisions.

Changing your character - Who you are as a person has changed. You may dress differently or speak differently to appease someone else. You do things you never would have done before and doubt your own reasons for not doing them previously.

Symptoms of manipulation are things that are elicited from you. They do not originate within you, they come from outside. Recognizing them is problematic because they can mimic your own naturally occurring emotions.

In order to delineate between your emotions and the ones artificially implanted in you, you need to look at why you feel the way you do. What caused a particular feeling? Do you feel shame because of something you did or a thought you had, or did someone say something or do something that made you feel ashamed? If you have changed the way you look, why did you change? Did you want to look this way or did someone else push you to do it?

It may also help to look at the effects of changes in your life. Is someone else benefitting from them? Are the changes hurting you financially, emotionally, or negatively impacting your health?

Finally, on some level, you know you are being abused. When you have to deal with the person who is manipulating you, you do not look forward to it. You feel unease and trepidation. You don't want to engage with them, but you do because you feel obligated because of guilt, fear, or just wanting to make them happy. But your unconscious mind knows that they are bad news, and it tries to tell you to stay away using emotion.

The manipulator wants you to believe these emotions are caused by something else that gives them an advantage over you.

Who are the Manipulators?

Anyone can be a manipulator. They are relatives, friends, co-workers, and partners. Some are master manipulators that hone their skills on every person they meet that has something they want. Others are well-meaning, and may not even consciously know they are doing it.

What drives someone to become a manipulator is somewhat complex. It seems that fear, self-loathing, fear of inadequacy and low self-esteem play a large role in shaping them. In other words, they use many of the same negative emotions to control you that they themselves can't deal with. It might be that submitting someone else to the emotional torment that they feel is a way to soothe their own pain. At the very least, they get a sense of empowerment from controlling others.

Most emotional manipulators fall into one of three groups: Narcissists, Psychopaths, and Sociopaths. Psychopaths are people with the inability to feel emotions like normal people. They are this way from birth and don't really understand emotions until they learn to recognize them in others and use them for their own benefit. Sociopaths experience emotions normally but have had to turn them off, usually due to trauma and/or abuse. Narcissists feel emotions, but don't care about anyone but themselves. They may recognize that you have emotions, but they come first and if you get hurt, too bad.

That is not to say that all manipulators are dangerously mentally ill, some are, but they are at the extreme end of a continuum of mental health. At the other end are functioning moderately affected people who may only represent a mild annoyance rather than a life-threatening scenario. There is a wide range in how manipulative and how dangerous they can be.

What the three groups do have in common is that they don't care much about other people's feelings beyond being able to use them for control. How you feel or what negative effect they have on you is not a concern for them. The damage they do is somebody else's problem. More often than not, they will put the blame for anything they do on you or someone else.

There are several distinct types of emotional manipulation. They can be separated into the categories **Aggressive and Passive-Aggressive**.

It is common for an abuser to only use one type of manipulation. But there is no limit. One person can play any or all the different types and change them like an actor changes costumes.

The following are the

Types of aggressive manipulation:

Screamer - Extreme flashes of anger, sometimes out of the blue are the modus operandi for this type of abuser. When confronted about almost anything, they react in a burst of rage meant to intimidate so they can take control of the situation, or deflect away from the topic that they didn't like being brought up. They may tell you that you are the problem and that you made them justifiably angry by saying anything at all. Or, they may rage about being the victim of a conspiracy or other force that is beyond their control.

Overt Intimidator - Like the Screamer with the intent to scare their victims into submission. The threats of violence are usually followed by blaming the victim for causing the episode. These are the easy manipulators to discover.

Blamer - They blame all their problems and behavior on others. They will project their motives on other people. They accuse you of stealing when they have been caught stealing from you. They give away their own motivations and deepest thoughts by accusing others of having them.

Nitpicker - Everything you do is wrong or at least could be done better. You drive too slowly, you dress poorly, and you don't even brush your teeth correctly! The Nitpicker attacks you relentlessly. Nothing is too inconsequential to mention and criticize. Nitpicking is a way for the manipulator to Show dominance over you in every arena. Like blaming, nitpicking is meant to blur reality and change what you believe to what they want you to believe.

Charmer - Charmers sweep you off your feet with compliments and even gifts. They give you all the attention you could want, for a little while, and then they change and become distant and never praise you. Their victims are left to think they caused this person to stop being caring and giving and should now do whatever it takes to make them happy again.

Ruiner - They always steal your thunder. They have a story similar to the one you just told, but better. Bigger and funnier or scarier. If you tell them you were in a fender-bender on the way to work, they will tell you they were in a 10-car pileup. Your anecdotes and opinions are overshadowed or lost completely.

Sexy Conspirator - They are sexually forward and want to sneak off with you for a discreet affair. They downplay their promiscuity as just having a little meaningless fun but then brag about breaking up other relationships with affairs. They try to gain power over you through sex and then use it to blackmail you when they don't get their way or are just tired of you. They leave a trail of broken relationships in their wake and will try to derail yours if you let them.

And the following are the

<u>Types of Passive-aggressive abuser:</u>

Liar - They use whatever tricks they can to warp the meaning of your words and use them against you. They don't lie directly, they lie by omission-where they give enough information to paint the picture they want you to see, but leave out crucial information that doesn't fit their agenda. They pretend to misunderstand and employ gossip and innuendo to attack their victims. When caught in a lie, they will alter their story and claim to have been misrepresented.

Victim - the professional victim will always play on your pity and guilt. The world has dealt them a bum hand over and over and over again, and they need you to help them. They can't survive without you, and if you don't help them, then their suffering is your fault. They start fights and cause problems and then lie and distort the situation to make they look like the victim. They are primarily motivated by fear and anger centered on their inability to achieve goals.

Helpless - Like the victim type, the "helpless" manipulator plays on your guilt and pity. The difference is that the relationships they form are open about their complete dependence on others. They cannot do for themselves and need you in order to get by. They may use charm and be effusive in their gratitude for your help but will turn and get nasty if you let them down. They feel they have entitled the help and support of others no matter the hardship it may cause.

There are also some manipulators who don't fit into any one category, they change their tactics based on the individual they are targeting. These are the super manipulators. They study and hone their craft and modify the attack on you on the fly. These are predators, and they are not limited to targets whose characteristics match up to his/her favored tactics. Anyone is a potential target for them. They have many of the skills that spies and other covert agents possess.

As soon as you find out what emotional manipulation is, you start to see how prevalent it is. You see it everywhere, people already in your life and people you just met. Mostly, however, you'll see it in advertising. Every single advertisement you see is playing on your emotions to get you to buy their products. These tactics that are used by ad agencies are much the same as the ones employed by the manipulative people in our lives. Emotional manipulation is so prevalent, that once you start to see it, you start to recognize similarities and patterns between advertisements and the things people subject each other to change behavior. Advertisements subtly tell you are overweight and otherwise unattractive by only showing pictures of perfectly sculpted models and actors. They make you feel insecure about yourself so that you will buy their products and that you won't be undesirable anymore. Your significant other may do the same thing to you by always pointing out people they are attracted to so you feel bad about how you look. Once you start to see how they work, you start you see the tactics they are using on you.

How To Use The Technique

Here is how you can try it out:

- Be clear on your end goal and talk about it indirectly in the form of songs, suggestions and movies. For instance, if you wish for your partner to take you on a vacation, sing songs on holidays over and over again; or talk about how all your friends are going on exotic vacations.

- Talk about your goal to yourself, sometimes even softly muttering to yourself and then when your target inquires you about it, say it is nothing.

- Put up images and wall art related to your end goal in your room and house if you and your target live together.

- Watch movies and shows that are related to your goal, especially when your target is around.

- After a few days of practicing subliminal influence, bring up the desired topic and your target will agree to what you want.

Ensure that you stay on your guard when carrying out these techniques so the other person does not influence you.

CHAPTER 5: Mental manipulation in everyday life: best secrets

As you work your way through the techniques discussed in the previous chapters, here are a few more dark psychology tactics you can add to your plan to influence people just like you please.

Fatigue Inducement

Also known as exhaustion manipulation, enervation manipulation and fatigue control, 'fatigue inducement' better known as 'mental fatigue inducement' is a manipulative technique that allows you to control your subject by exhausting him/ her emotionally.

Physical fatigue refers to the transient inability of your body and the muscles in it to work at their optimal level. Similarly, mental fatigue refers to the incapability of your mind to work optimally.

When you feel mentally fatigued, you feel swamped emotionally and psychologically and oftentimes surrender to what the other person wants just to save yourself from more exhaustion.

You need to put this very information to use in order to mentally exhaust someone you wish to manipulate.

How To Use The Technique

Here is how you can mentally tire someone.

- Act nicely with your subject so he/ she doesn't suspect your ulterior motives and doubt your intentions.

- After some time, bring up a topic that's the bone of contention between the two of you and constantly talk about how that has upset you, but you are ready to make the compromise just to show your love for that person. If you keep talking about your pain, there will come a point when the other person becomes frustrated and agrees to do as you want.

- You can also bring up a memory or an instance when you did something just to please the other person and how that affected your life negatively, but you chose to move on just to please him.

- You can also constantly criticize the other person, talk about his/ her failures and blame him/ her for the problems you face to emotionally upset and exhaust him/ her.

When you keep doing that for a while, there comes a point when your subject succumbs to your will and agrees to do as you want.

When you try to emotionally drain your target, make sure to act upset yourself and as the person going through the hard time so he/ she is unable to focus on his/ her own wellbeing.

Choice Restriction

This is another technique that very slyly makes you manipulate others to do everything according to your desires by providing them with limited choices, but not the one they would like to make themselves.

To use this technique, you need to first be aware of your intentions and goal as well as the wants of the target with respect to the topic of interest.

Once you are aware of that, you need to present your target with a few choices, making sure to exclude the one he/ she would like to opt for so he/ she is forced to do as you want.

How To Use The Technique

Here's how you can work on this strategy:

- Be clear on the issue you wish your subject to agree to, his/ her desires and intentions as well as your goals.

- Next, you need to weigh out the pros and cons of the choice your target would like to make so you can highlight the cons if the topic comes up.

- Brush up your knowledge on the pros of your choice and also think of a few other choices that you can offer your subject. Make sure they are not as good as the one you would suggest.

- Bring up the topic while conversing to your subject quickly jumping to the conclusion and listing down the choices you have already identified.

- Time and again, talk about how a certain option (your preferred choice) is the best one and how it aligns with what your target wants. Even if it is completely opposite to his/ her desire, if you repeatedly tell him/ her that the option is what they want, they will eventually agree to it.

- Do not insinuate at any point that you have interest in the option you are constantly suggesting to them and let them know that the choice is theirs. Soon enough, your target will agree to what you want.

When practicing this technique, be prepared to offer an argument against your target's preferred choice if the topic comes up.

Subliminal Influence

Subliminal influence entails giving someone messages and suggestions camouflaged in some music, joke, jingles or other ideas to imbed your desired idea into your target's mind.

The human brain is designed to react to things exactly how they come.

When there are certain ideas imbedded in your mind time and again, they become rooted in it and then influence your thought process, attitude, behavior and decisions.

You need to use this knowledge to your advantage to influence people to do whatever it is you want.

Techniques of Manipulation

Everyone in the world has likely used manipulation at some points in their lives. This could have been through telling the most straightforward lies to get out of situations or by flirting with others to get what you want. In understanding the techniques used by manipulators in their work, you need to ask yourself the following question:

Who is at threat from a manipulator? To regulate their victims, the pullers of the strings (manipulators) use several tactics, but most importantly, they do this by targeting specific kinds of personalities. You are more likely to be a victim of manipulation if you have low self- esteem, if you are inexperienced, pleased easily, if you are not confident about yourself and if you lack assertive instincts.

What are the requirements for successful manipulation? Primarily, successful manipulation encompasses a manipulator. Manipulation is also likely to be achieved through covert hostile methods. For successful persuasion, a manipulator has to:

- Cover their violent purposes, deeds, and be friendly.
- Be aware of the psychological susceptibilities of the targeted person so as to conclude which strategies are likely to be the most effective.
- Have an adequate level of callousness to have no doubts about triggering injury to the victim if necessary.

The manipulators exploit different defenselessness habits that exist in the victim's character and such include:

- The naïveté of the targeted person - Based on naïveté, the targeted person experiences hardships to buy the notion that many human beings are always sneaky, deceitful, and hard-nosed. This means if you are the victim, you will be in denial that you are being victimized.
- If you are over-conscientiousness - This is where you find yourself ready to grant the exploiter the advantage of distrust. The

manipulator ends up blaming you and supporting their side, which makes you trust them easily. If you are too honest, you end up thinking everyone else is reliable as well.

- Self-confidence - Controllers often check whether you are a self-doubting person and whether you lack self-assertiveness, and this makes you go into a defensive mode effortlessly. You end up not giving a second thought about errors.

- Over-intellectualization - This makes it hard for you to understand and therefore, you end up believing your manipulator's reasons for being hurtful.

- Your emotional reliance - If you have a submissive personality, you are more likely to be a victim of manipulation. The more you rely on your emotions, the more vulnerable you are to being manipulated.

- Loneliness - If you are a lonely person, you are likely to agree to take little proposals of social interaction. Some manipulators will propose being your companion, but at a price. This also involves being narcissistic whereby, you fall easily for any kind of unjustified flattery. Lonely people act without any consultations. Therefore, loneliness goes hand in hand with being impulsive.

- Materialistic - Having a get-rich-quick mindset makes you cheap prey for manipulators. This means you are greedy and want to get rich quickly, hence end up acting immorally for some sort of material exchange.

- The elderly are also at a higher risk of getting controlled easily because they are fatigued and not able to multitask. Likelihoods the elderly will have a thought that a manipulator might be a conman are very rare. Manipulators thus take advantage of them and commit elder abuse.

Techniques of Manipulation

Manipulators take time to explore and examine your characteristics and find out how vulnerable you are to exploitation. They tend to control their victims by playing with their psychological characters. Having read the points above, now you need to know what the tactics and techniques are manipulators use to control their victims. They include various methods, as discussed below.

Techniques of manipulation

Reinforcement: This can be either positive, negative, or intermittent forms of reinforcement.

> i. **Positive reinforcement**: This involves the case where the manipulator uses praises, charms, crocodile tears, unnecessary apologizing, public acknowledgment, cash, presents, consideration, and facial languages like forced laughter or smiles.
>
> ii. **Negative reinforcement**: A manipulator removes you from a negative situation as a favor.
>
> iii. **Intermittent reinforcement**: This is also known as partial reinforcement. This creates an environment full of fear and doubts. It encourages the victim of manipulation to persist.

Punishment: The manipulator acts in a nagging manner. There is yelling, silent treatment, intimidating behavior, and threatening of the victim. Manipulators cry and tend to play the victim card, thus emotionally blackmailing the victim and can go further by swearing they are the innocent one.

Lying: it entails two ways; lying by commission and lying by omission.

    i. Lying by commission - You will find it hard to tell when a manipulator is lying the moment they do it, and the truth won't reveal itself until it is too late. You should understand that some people are experts at lying and thus you should not give in easily to their tactics.

    ii. Lying by omission - This is a subtle way used to manipulate, and it entails telling lies, and at the same time, withholding significant amounts of the facts. It is also applied in propaganda.

Denial: Manipulators rarely admit they are wrong. Even when they have done something wrong, they will refuse to believe it. They are rational and always assert that their behavior is not harmful or they are not as bad as someone else has explained. They accompany every exploitation with phrases like, 'it was only a joke'.

Attention: This includes selective inattention and attention. In this case, manipulators deliberately refuse to listen or pay attention to anything that distracts them from their agendas. They always defend themselves with phrases like, 'I do not need to listen to that'.

Deviation: Controllers never answer any questions directly and always steer the discussion to another topic. If not so, the manipulator gives irrelevant or rogue answers to the direct questions asked.

Intimidation: In this case, the manipulator applies two methods of intimidation; covert intimidation and guilt trip. In underground extortion, the manipulators throw their targets onto the self-justifying side through the use of implied threats. A guilt trip is a technique where the manipulator tries to suggest to the meticulous prey that they no longer care and this makes the victim feel bad and they start doubting themselves, hence, they find themselves in a submissive position.

Use of Sarcasm: The manipulator shames the victim by using put-downs and sarcasm that makes the victim doubt themselves. Making the victim feel unworthy gives an entry for the manipulator to defer the victim. These shaming tactics may include fierce glances, unpleasant tones, rhetorical comments or questions, and subtle sarcasm. Some of the victims end up not daring to challenge the manipulator as it fosters a sagacity of meagerness to their targets.

Belittling their Target: Manipulators use this technique to put their target on the self-justifying side, while at the same time, covering the belligerent aims of the persuader. The persuader then misleadingly blames their target in response to the victim's defensive mechanisms. This also involves the case where a manipulator plays the victim role by portraying themselves as victims of circumstances to gain sympathy, thereby, getting what they want. This technique aims at the caring and compassionate victims as they cannot stand seeing someone suffer, and thus, the manipulator takes that chance to get the victim's cooperation.

Seduction: In this case, the manipulator uses praise or any form of flattery, which involves supporting the victim to gain their conviction. Manipulators can even start helping you to increase your loyalty, and it will be hard for you to suspect their ill intents. The manipulator can as well play the servant role where their actions will be justified by phrases such as, 'I am just doing my job' or 'I am in service to a certain authority figure.' In this case, the victim will give their trust and end up being manipulated.

Feigning: Manipulator pretends that any harm caused was unintentional or they are being accused falsely. Manipulators often wear a surprised face, hence making the victim question their own sanity. Feigning also involves the case where the manipulator plays dumb and pretends they are totally unaware of what the victim is talking about. The victim starts doubting themselves while the manipulator continues to point out the main ideas they included just in case there is any doubt. This happens only if the manipulator had used cohorts in advance that helps them in backing up their stories.

Brandishing anger: The manipulator shows off how angry they are in order to intensify the victim's shock to get their submission. In the real sense, the manipulator is never angry, but they act like they are, especially when denied access to what they want. A manipulator can as well control their anger to avoid any confrontations or hide their intents.

Manipulators often threaten the victims by saying they are going to report the cases to the police. Anger is a way of blackmailing the victim to avoid telling the truth, as it wards off any further inquiries. This makes the victim focus more on the anger of the manipulator rather than on the manipulation technique being used.

The Bandwagon effect: This is the case where the manipulator tends to comfort the victim by claiming that, whether right or wrong, many people have already done some things, and thus, the victim should do it anyway. The manipulator uses phrases like 'Many people like you…' This kind of manipulation is mainly applied to those under peer pressure conditions. Similar cases are when a manipulator tries to lure the victim into taking drugs or abusing other substances.

The techniques discussed above are the tested and proven tactics that any manipulator will strive to use to get a strong control of their victims. Before a manipulator persuades their victims, there are those steps they have to follow to make sure they fully control their victim's minds.

Whatever the reasons for manipulating someone, you should always play your cards safely. That is why you should learn how to manage and control the thoughts of people, the strategies, and steps you need to use in various situations. There are three authentic manipulating skills you can learn quickly through the steps discussed below. If you want to manipulate others in an easy way, come on! Shed a fake tear and follow the following steps.

Effective Steps of Manipulation

Honing Your Persuasion
Skills

I. **Take an Acting Class**: If you want to be a manipulator, you first need to learn how to master your emotions and make others interested in your forced feelings. Now, if you desire to look more distressed that you really are or even want to apply a variety of emotional techniques to get what you want, then take an acting class since it will improve your persuasion powers. When considering an acting class, you need to note you should never tell people you are taking a drama class if you are learning how to persuade and control people's minds. This is because they may get suspicious over your skills rather than believing in you.

II. **Taking a Debate Class**: After you have taken acting classes and learned how to master your emotions when convincing others to get what you want, you need to take debate classes, which might also involve public speaking classes to learn more on organizing, presenting what you think and making you sound more convincing.

III. **Pacing**: In this step, you will learn how to establish similarities. You need to learn how to mirror your victim's body language, then see how effective you can control your tonal variations and other body languages. The gentle and manipulative technique is the best when persuading your employer or fellow employees to get them do something for you. In this case, you should NEVER be emotional since this is a professional setting.

IV. **Be Charismatic**: Once you are charismatic, you will have the tendency to get what you want. In this step, you need to learn how to smile and light up a room. You should as well have approachable body gestures so your targeted people feel willing to talk to you. You should be flexible such that you can hold up a discussion with anyone despite their age, body size, or profession. The following are other techniques you should apply to be charismatic:

- Making others feel special by maintaining eye contact when talking to them, asking them how they feel and what are their interests. Show them how much you care about knowing them even if you know you do not mean it.

- Love yourself and what you do by exuding your confidence. Have faith in yourself so others can take you seriously and fall into your persuasion intent.

- Be confident even if what you are saying is true or false. When speaking, be glib as this makes your target fall into your purpose easily.

V. **Learn from Other Manipulators**: Since you are still an amateur, you need to learn more from the masters. Look for your friends or family members who are persuasion masters and take notes. This helps in getting new insights on how to persuade and influence people even if it means you end up being a manipulation victim. If you are interested in the art of mind control, you might also find yourself manipulating one of the masters.

VI. **Read People**: You should also learn to read people as everyone has a different emotional and psychological composition and should, therefore, be persuaded for various purposes. Before you apply your latest manipulation skills, take time to learn your target by understanding what makes them tick, then evaluate which approach suits them. The following are the most proven factors you will come across when getting to know more about people:

- The majority are vulnerable to emotional responses. They are emotional themselves as they can cry while or after watching a movie; they love pets and are sympathetic. This means in order for you to persuade them, you will have to play with their emotions until they empathize and sympathize with you and give in to your intents.
- Others were raised in authoritarian backgrounds, hence have a guilt reflex. Since they are used to getting punished for every little wrong deed, they grow up feeling guilty about anything they do. As a manipulator, make them feel guilty for not fulfilling your

demands, and within no time, they will grant your wishes.

- Other people are amenable to rational approaches. They are always logical-minded, tend to read the news every day, and they always ask for facts before deciding on anything. In this case, you will need to apply your calm mind-controlling powers to influence these people rather than using your emotions.

CHAPTER 6: 10 best mental manipulation techniques used on prisoners of war

Emotionally intelligent people don't harass their staff or bully their colleagues. They understand how to obtain others to accomplish what they need without resolving to arrogance or aggression. Being versatile and open to suggestion, they make great leaders or colleagues.

People easily open up to you

Being empathic, emotionally smart people can listen in to others' emotions, so they easily understand others' point of view or the conditions which may have led them to do certain things.

You certainly are a master of your feelings in any situation

The ability to identify, understand, and manage your emotions means you'll continually be a step forward over others with regards to responding to challenging situations. Besides, getting responsible for your emotions can help you manage stress better.

You resolve conflicts easily

The secret to successfully resolving conflicts is to deal with them prior to the situation gets beyond control. Your ability to manage your emotions, and conveniently understand those of others, along with triggers that may possess led to them, makes it possible to respond to someone's behavior in a manner that will diffuse a potentially difficult situation.

Because your interpersonal skills are good, you feel relaxed around people and so are not quickly thrown off balance in unpredictable and difficult situations, or with unfriendly or hostile individuals openly.

You easily turn into a leader

Emotionally intelligent folks have the majority of the traits of highly effective leaders: they are empathic, confident, communicative, positive, and supportive.

You can work anywhere, with anyone

Great people skills, empathy, and social awareness imply that you will be able to work well and get most from every situation even under difficult circumstances or in a foreign culture.

You get yourself a high-paid job easily

Being probably the most sought-after abilities at work, high emotional cleverness can help you get the job of your dreams.

You don't carry out or say things you later regret

Knowing that you need to understand and process your feelings before releasing them, implies that you will only act once you've had an opportunity to consider the problem. Sometimes, all it takes is having a few minutes to believe things over and present yourself a chance to calm down and measure the circumstance, before making the final decision.

If there are occasions you are too embarrassed to take into account because of what you said, or did, it's probably because at the time you didn't have or didn't use your emotional cleverness, as a total consequence of which you made decisions you resided to regret.

You are a valued friend and confidant

Psychological intelligence skills are as useful outside work just, as some of your most significant emotions and decisions happen outside the workplace, eg with your family, in your passionate relationships, together with your friends, children, etc.

You are fulfilled

Having a successful career and being accomplished personally means you should have lived your life to the fullest.

So, through inside your feelings, behavior, and interpersonal relations, emotional intelligence includes a major effect on the standard of your life.

To continually cultivate and enhance these skills, you should never go wrong on your:

Self-awareness

Be constantly in touch with your feelings and figure out how to listen in to them.

Social skills

Cultivate your communication abilities rather than underestimate the charged power of words. Besides, to become highly empathic, you possess to try to develop humility. Although becoming humble isn't easy in a society which encourages individuality and competition, ability to admit your limitations and mistakes openly, are characteristics of a true leader.

Emotional regulation

Figure out how to control your strong emotions, particularly negative ones, and never act on impulse. Practice this by thinking about something that will make you feel hurt, angry, or exploited. Sit down with the feeling, feel the humiliation, or anger, "digest" it, and only once you have calmed down "respond" to the individual or scenario that made you are feeling that way.

CHAPTER 7: How to recognize the manipulation in the sale: best tricks

Now we are going to look at some tools and techniques that have proven themselves to be the most powerful and successful with manipulation. Some of this will be a review because of what we have already looked at. Don't worry about that. Reviewing is good. Practice makes permanent. We'll look at some examples as well to see how it all works together.

Remember what we discussed about sales because this isn't to suggest in any way that salespeople are bad. They are not usually bad. Ideally, after a sale of whatever it may be, there are two winners. The salesperson won by making the sale and the customer won by acquiring what they wanted. Regardless, there are certain tactics used in sales that help with the transaction process. Here are examples of these and how they work to influence the customer.

It's a good idea that we remember what traits and characteristics good manipulators must possess prior to any manipulation. As a review, they must be intelligent. There are so many different factors that will determine the outcome of any sales exchange and the salesperson must be well versed with all of them. Of course, they need charisma. Most people are not going to purchase anything from a true asshole. There may be an exception if what they need is a matter of life and death, but that's about it. He or she also needs to be an expert at knowing and reading others. They need to be able to shift gears in the conversation at any time. The sales person needs to control the conversation but not be forceful in doing so. They can't be bullies. Another key trait is they need to at least appear like they know what it is they are talking about or selling, to the customer. Portraying an image of knowing what you are talking about leads the other person to have confidence in you and willingness to trust your word.

Studies have shown that one important trait that a manipulator need possess is likeness. There is a name for this technique and it's called "liking." What this is saying is that a person is much more apt to buy from, agree with, or obey someone with whom they feel likeness. If you were going to buy a vehicle and went to the car dealership. There are 3 different sales people to choose from. One of them is about your age, dresses the same as you, and you perceive that person to be attractive, you will choose that person. Other factors are things such as race, sex, and geographical origin. The other two salespeople may have more experience, can handle the transaction more quickly, or possibly be able to offer a better deal and all of that probably won't matter. Good and knowledgeable manipulators know this and use it to their advantage.

Another good ability to have is to always at least appear to know about what it is you are selling or doing. Whether or not you really have the knowledge isn't as important as the ability to portray to others that you do. One part of this is being able to dress for the occasion. If you are going to interact with a suit-wearing professional, you should be able to dress and act that way. If you are going to work with someone who looks down on such types of people, you should be able to act the same then too. I had a friend who was a car salesman. He wore a shirt and tie to work each day with dress pants. However, he always had a pair of jeans and cowboy boots with him. If he knew that there was a farmer, or someone of the sort, coming he would change clothes as soon as he could. He was also the top salesperson at his place of business consistently every year.

The two previous tactics, liking and confidence, are great but there are many more. What we are now discussing, primarily deal with sales but there are other times where they can be put to use. As with everything in life, it's all situational. Intelligent people know and understand this and are able to tweak whatever they need to when the time comes for them to do so. Let's look at a way to manipulate someone into really wanting, or believing they need, something they otherwise wouldn't think so highly of. How do we make someone believe anything to be of more value than it really is? It's possible to do this by making everyone around them want the same thing, but that would be exhausting. It's scary to think about just how time-consuming an attempt like that could be. Thankfully, there is a much easier way to do this. That's creating, what is known as, a fear of loss. This is one of the most common tactics that any salesperson uses. What is it?

Creating a fear of loss plays on basic psychology principles. That is, people place a higher value on things which they believe are in limited supply. Have you ever seen a "limited edition" of some kind of vehicle? Have you ever heard this statement; "hurry here because supplies are limited?" Actually, everything that is manufactured is in some limited supply. Even if there are billions of them, the supply is limited. However, just hearing the word limited triggers something in our minds that tells us the object has more worth than it really does. Back to cars, here is a true story.

When I went to purchase my first, self-bought vehicle, I went somewhere where one of my best friend's father was the manager. He knew me and therefore knew those in which I felt that I was somehow in competition with. I was always into sports and very competitive by nature. I wanted a Chevrolet K-5 Blazer. My friend's dad came over to me and told me that the last year they were making that model was the same year and there were only 2 more left. One of those had already been ordered by a boy that I had always been in competition with. He told me that if I didn't get that exact vehicle, I would never have one and then the other boy would have one and I never could. I'd like to point out that everything that I was told was true. He didn't lie to me as that is not a good thing for any salesperson to do. He was able to use his knowledge of me and the fear of loss to lead me into my decision. Did it work? I drove that thing almost until it fell apart.

Lastly, here we are going to discuss, what is known as, the illusion of choice. What this means is we are making the other believe that he or she has control over his or her decision, which is true, but we are asking questions which lead that person in a particular direction. This is also a way to limit the number of possible choices a person is likely to make. Here is an example. You want your non-compliant teenager to do a chore. You need him to vacuum his room. You can tell him to do it but will be met with resistance and will just make the mood of the day terrible. He has agreed to help with one thing around the house, so you want to get him to vacuum his room. He hates doing that and you want to think of a sly way in which to get him to do it. More than vacuuming his room, he detests doing laundry in any amount. Doing one load of laundry, to him, feels like having his teeth pulled out with plyers. The solution is simple. You ask "would you rather vacuum your room or do the laundry?" You have given him a sense of control and have limited the possible answers to one of the two, but you know that he is going to choose to vacuum. He will think that he has avoided doing laundry and that will trump his thought process only being on the fact that he is doing something that he hates. A person believing that he or she has a right to choose is one of the best motivators available. People need, and strongly desire, to have importance and worth and these plays of this need.

Another tactic that can be applied here is what is known as the "commitment and consistency" technique. This is basically the same as knowing someone and then using that knowledge in your manipulation of them. Here, you take what you know about the person and use those things. You base what you believe he or she will do on what has been done in the past. If history provides something beneficial to your situation, you can use it to your benefit. If history has shown the person to do something that you don't want them to do, you can use this knowledge to navigate the person away from that decision well before that point arrives.

It's important that we discuss the difference between manipulation and persuasion. Many people believe them both to be synonymous, but they are far from the same. Both can be used to manipulate someone but using persuasion isn't the same as manipulating. The process may be the same but the intentions of the person doing the manipulating, or the persuading, is different. Here is the key difference. If the one doing the persuading has the best interest in the other in mind, what is being done is persuasion. On the flip side, if he or she only has his or her chosen outcome, regardless of what happens to the other, in mind, that is manipulation. Look at sales. That is a process of persuasion. The salesperson has his customer's best interest in mind, as well as his own, when leading the transaction. Therefore, it's persuasion. If the same salesperson only cared about his outcome and is planning on ripping his customer off, that's manipulation.

Favors can also be great tools for manipulation. This does require a pre-existing relationship with the person you are trying to manipulate. First, there is the reciprocity method. This is basically asking for repayment of a past favor that you have done for the person you are trying to lead. This can have been done directly or otherwise. As long as he or she believes that you are responsible for that favor, you are good at using it. Asking for repayment can also be indirect if need be. Using what one would call a "guilt trip" can work here. If you believe that the person is going to be hesitant in going along with the repayment, you can say something like this. "It sure was hard doing that for you." Maybe be less direct, but this is a baseline for you to use.

Reciprocity usually is a 1+1 deal meaning you can't ask for a mountain if you gave an ant hill. You can step this up a notch though. Asking for larger favors is acceptable as long as it's not a large increase. Tact is something that is needed here. Knowing how far to push things and when to stop is something you must know, and be able to do, before ever using this method. That is, unless you are willing to go straight to the demand phase should it fail. If you are able to read people well, have a history working with the specific individual you are manipulating, and you have a specific goal with the interaction, you can barter favors and this will work well in most cases.

One of the most powerful tools that can be utilized in manipulation is also another tactic based on basic psychology. This is similar to what we discussed about likeness. Just like people are inclined to deal with someone they believe they have commonalities with, social proof can also be used. This was something we discussed at the beginning of this book. What is social proof? It's peer pressure. When it comes to sales, social proof may be all that is required. With other kinds of manipulation, it makes things much easier. People are subconsciously (unaware) of this process.

They are unknowingly influenced by others and this can be very strong in nature. There are many reasons why this happens. Reputation, or fear of loss of reputation, guilt, envy, etc. are examples. This isn't limited to what others may have but also by what they do. It's a human trait that can be used both in a negative way or in a positive. You can apply this in your manipulating covertly, or you can overtly. One way in which you can use this openly is like this. You want your subject, he or she you are manipulating, to do something. Just tell them that someone you know they dislike does not approve of doing it. "John hates it when this is done. Can you help me out by doing it?"

Next, there is the use of authority in manipulation. There was a study, called the "Milgram Experiment," done at Yale in 1963. Stanley Milgram, a psychologist there, was studying genocide committed during World War 2. Without going into detail about the experiment, what it determined was that people are much more likely to follow the instructions of someone they perceive as being in power. "The white coat" effect is what is meant here. If you were in a hospital and put on a white coat, you could walk up to anyone and they would believe you to be knowledgeable of what you tell them and they will be inclined to follow your orders. This is a basic summary, but there is information on this particular study available. Remember this. What someone believes is their perception, or their truth, and is all that is needed for manipulation to take place with them.

Just as powerful as techniques involving one's perception of others, like peer-pressure, is a person's emotions. You can manipulate people easily and in many different areas playing on their emotions. This does not always have to be with bad intentions. There are negative parts of it though and here is one example. Playing on someone's negative emotions or threatening to trigger them in manipulating that person. This is commonly done using fear as the emotion. Fear of keeping something from happening, or fear of punishment, are strong motivators. Fear of loss is also strong. In math, 1+1=2. The same principle can be used here with emotions. If one emotional trigger is strong, adding another will double the possibility of success. This is more on the malicious front and shouldn't be applied to manipulation by normal people.

For the purposes of information, here is what is meant by the 1+1 method. You are a horrible and deviant person. You are, for all purposes, a sociopath and you have decided that you want someone that is close to you to do something which he or she does not want to do. You have no problems with emotionally harming those who love you because you have no compassion and can ignore any little voice popping up in your head calling you a multitude of dirty words. So, you are going to do your damage. If you are close to the person, you should know them well. You should know of something that will trigger an emotion which will devastate that person. Both you and that person know what it will do and you are going to use it. You also know of someone that person loves and protects and you are going to use that too. Let's use a child as an example here. You want the mother to do something and she is resisting your request, or demand, and you have had enough being civil. Let's add here that you are the biological father of that child. Tell the mother that if she does not comply, you are going to take the child and never allow her to see him again. If the two of you are together, which hopefully given your personality and character flaws, isn't the case, you are threatening to take several things and playing on multiple emotional triggers. First, she faces losing you. She also faces losing the child. Finally, she faces never seeing her child again. Regardless of whether or not you are actually capable of carrying this out successfully, she is probably going to comply with your demands and this is out of the emotional fear of loss.

Now that we have taken a look at the dark side, let's return to the white and gray areas of manipulation or persuasion. Another tactic which can be useful is reinforcement. Here is another tactic that can go either way. It can also be carried out in either a negative or positive way. Anyone who is a parent, or took psychology 101 in school, will know what this is. It's a guaranteed result of a reaction or decision. A positive reinforcement is a reward. Your child gets an "A" on his report card, so you buy him a candy bar. The other side of this is negative reinforcement or punishment. Your child gets a failing grade, so you ground him for an amount of time. Either may work. A person may choose something knowing they will get a reward for doing so. He or she may also choose it because of knowing what bad thing will happen if it's not chosen. Key factors in using this are the person's personality and values, his or her goals and fears, and what is being offered or threatened.

Those who are most successful at manipulating others use an arsenal of tactics. As we have learned, they also have the needed characteristics and abilities to become a good manipulator and have learned the techniques and how to read others to the point they are almost able to correctly guess anyone's next word or move. They are able to adapt to any situation or personality in which they are faced with and can alter their own personas when needed. There is an order of elements needed to manipulate and these are all a must. There is no skipping around. If a person is trying to learn to manipulate and he or she attempts to skip any step, or lacks just one characteristic, that person is likely to fail.

CHAPTER 8: In-depth analysis of a politician: how do they manipulate us?

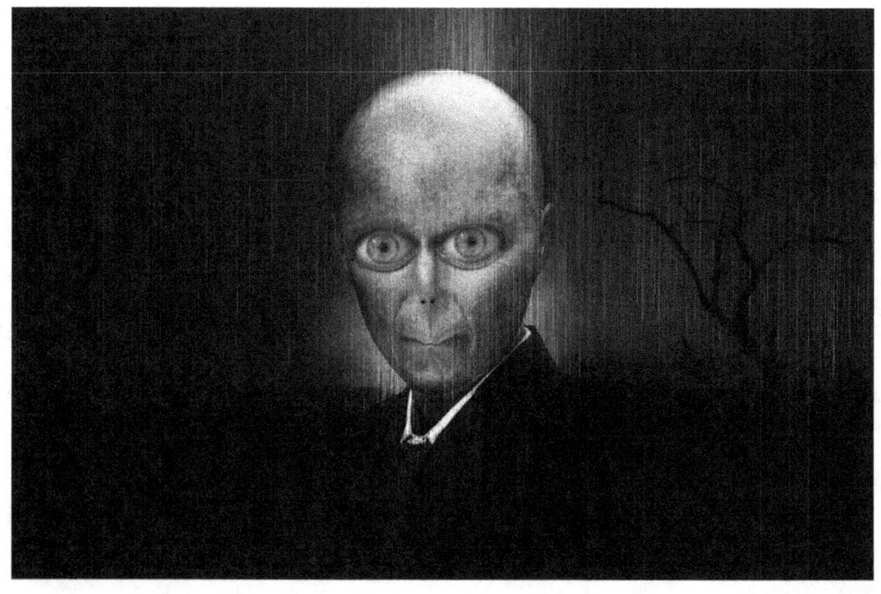

There are essentially two types of people in the world: leaders and followers.

Most people tend to be followers, predominantly because they either don't possess the skills to be leaders or they don't have the desire to have that level of responsibility on their shoulders.

Most of us have more than enough responsibility hanging over us every day. Going to work, taking care of children, paying bills, looking after family and friends, and so much more. How many times have you seen things in the news that you didn't like and wished you could change, but you knew you didn't have the time to get involved?

Some people are natural leaders, or more accurately, have a strong enough desire to be leaders that they learn the skills to be able to influence others.

So why do so many people allow themselves to be influenced? One of the key reasons is information. Even though we are currently in the most incredible age as far as information is concerned, people have limited knowledge about a wide range of topics. For so long, gaining unbiased knowledge about any topic required going to the library, looking up in the card catalog the right books to read, and sifting through the books to determine if it even had the right information they were looking for.

Today, all you have to do is Google search the topic and you are met with a wealth of information, most of it biased and inaccurate. This overwhelming amount of information is both a blessing and a curse. When people have to struggle to get information, or when they are overwhelmed with so many opposing viewpoints on certain topics, they tend to be more open to the opinions of others who **appear** to know what's best or what they're talking about.

People allow themselves to be influenced because it's often easier to listen to rational, well-reasoned thoughts and ideas from others.

In essence, most of us want to be influenced so that we can feel assured that we are doing the right thing in our lives, making the right decisions, and that alleviates a tremendous amount of stress.

Just think about the last time you were influenced by someone, whether it was a politician, a musician, an actor, a friend, parent, or anybody else. Why were you influenced? What was it that they did that influenced you?

Was it their passion?

Was it the information they possessed?

Was it there position in society?

Was it their name?

Was it their relationship to you?

Or was it because you found out on your own that what they were saying was factual?

People allow themselves to be influenced because it provides comfort. Being part of a team, even if it's only the illusion of a team, provides us the feeling of comfort in numbers. It is much more difficult, both mentally and physically, to achieve things or think that you can achieve things when you are alone or feel alone.

Now, do you want to be influenced or do you want to be the one to influence others?

CHAPTER 9: Take control of your life and manipulate whoever you want

Each one of us moves through the decision cycle when deciding something. The decision cycle comprises of 5 major predictable stages, which eventually lead you to make a certain decision which can be desired or even undesired. To be able to successfully influence people, you need to have an understanding of the decision cycle and then be able to identify the stage someone is on as well as the stage you are on so you can use the appropriate techniques and convince him/ her.

1.   Identify the Need and a Decision that Needs to be Made

This is the first stage of the decision making cycle when someone realizes he/she has a need for something and has to make a certain decision. At this stage, you need to be clear about the decision you wish to take so you take the right step forward and can influence the people involved in the decision effectively.

For instance, if you are being offered a great job, but you have to move to another state, you need to decide what will be the most appropriate decision for you and your family. Only then can be clear on the decision you wish to take that you can easily influence others too. If you are confused about it, you are quite likely to feel double minded and may not be able to convince someone else as well.

2.   Collect Enough Relevant Information

At this stage, you need to gather as much information as possible regarding the decision you wish to take so you can be sure of it and reach a more informed conclusion. Continuing with the earlier example of moving to another state to pursue a job, you need to gather information on the living expenses in that new state, education expenses of kids and other different factors that entail living there so that you can assess the pros and cons of shifting there and those of living in your current state. Once you have enough data, you can make the right decision for yourself and others involved in the decision.

When it comes to influencing someone who is on this stage, you need to present him/her with enough influential data so he/she is convinced of your decision. For instance, if you fear your partner may not agree to move to another state, you need to convince him/her by presenting him with all the evidences of how life will be better for your family there.

Similarly, if you wish for your friends to agree on something as simple as watching your choice of movie, collect as much information as you can on how that is the best movie to watch that night and how it will be exciting for everyone. In this scenario, the decision is that of watching a movie and the next step is to pick one. If your friends have agreed on watching a movie, you now need to supply them with the right kind of information to convince them to watch a film you want.

3. Identifying Different Alternatives Available and Evaluating Each

As you collect sufficient information to support your decision, you also need to start looking for different alternatives of that choice. This ensures that you make an informed decision instead of jumping for the first thing that catches your fancy.

When you present a certain solution or option to anybody, you would like to convince them to do a certain act and he/she is likely to look for any substitutes available for that option. Your job at this stage is to stay calm and instead of directly telling them how seeking alternatives is not a healthy approach, provide them with substitutes that aren't as good as your choice. Also, you can share the cons of the different alternatives they pick so they ultimately agree to do what you want.

For example, if you want your partner to go out on a picnic with you instead of a mountain hike that he/she is interested in, ask him/her to list down all the pros and cons of both the choices. You can also add in a splash of emotion and tell him/her of how sick you got the last time you went for a hike. As you do that, ensure that you do not make up any excuses, stories or false cons associated with his/her option. Instead, genuinely point out all the reasons why your choice is better.

4. Making a Choice

Once all the different options have been weighed against one another, you and the others involved in the decision are ready to reach a conclusion. When someone reaches this stage, you need to stay as poised as possible and make sure you keep your facial expressions as calm as possible. You must not flinch, twitch or make any expression that makes the other person feel uncomfortable or that his/her choice/decision is not good enough.

However, you also need to stick to your stance and make it clear that you feel it is the best decision for everyone. If you believe your team should select a certain marketing strategy that involves using social media instead of spending a hefty amount of money on billboard advertisement, state it clearly. If you are in a position to make the final call, do so. If, however, you are not in that position and have to somehow accept the decision that everyone agrees to make, do so gracefully without budging from the stance. When the time is right and others experience a setback due to their decision, inform them politely of how you suggested differently and that they should try what you suggested.

5. Review the Final Decision and Any Consequences Faced

This is the final stage of the process when you analyze the decision that was taken and assess whether or not it worked out well in your favor. If the decision failed to meet the need that was identified in the start, you need to take another decision. If you had agreed to do what the other person wanted, but the decision did not turn out to be beneficial, clearly paint the consequences to that person. It is likely they would now agree to do what you want.

A very effective technique to influence others is to let them have their way first especially if you are sure it would backfire. Once the outcome is not even, close to what they expect, you can gently barge in, rub in the fact that you had made a different suggestion and now is the time to try that out. The other person is likely to feel remorseful then and easily agree to what you want. Since he/she feels sorry for making the wrong decision, the likelihood of him/her agreeing to your decisions is quite high the next time around.

Following the decision making cycle and trying different strategies to sway the person at different stages of the cycle is one of the many ways to influence people. Let us now learn about using body language to manipulate others.

CONCLUSION

Throughout this book, we have discussed all of the things that are important to remember to avoid being manipulated, and to include positive persuasion in the way that you interact with others. It isn't something that is going to be achieved overnight, but with more and more practice, you can remember that you have what it takes to get the things that you desire most.

The biggest mistake that some will make after learning of these methods is to use them to only their advantage and take from others rather than spreading the happiness and satisfaction received through influence. It is a lot easier to negatively manipulate someone than to positively persuade them. Sometimes, persuasion means building trust.

Manipulation can simply mean instilling fear. While manipulation might be easier, it is going to cause a lot more difficult things in the end that you will have to clean up afterwards!

Remember that this process starts with really understanding someone's personality. There are common types of manipulators out there and you might be able to sense this personality trait in another person right away. Similarly, you will also recognize that there are hidden qualities that won't always emerge at first.

Remember to recognize that not all manipulative behaviors presented by an individual indicates that she is a malicious person. Having manipulative parents or long-term partners can rub off on our behavior, so we might sometimes say and do things that aren't meant to be manipulative but can come off that way. Always look at intention when determining if someone is really being manipulative or not.

Also, don't forget that body language can play a huge role in how someone will be perceived. You can start to see persuasive body language in others more often than you did before as soon as you become aware of what this kind of body language looks like. Ensure you are aware of your own body language as well so as not to be manipulated by others.

At the end of the day, manipulation is generally a way for a person to get the things that they desire most. We all have basic human needs and instincts that drive our behavior. If we are not careful with how we go about getting these things, we can hurt others. The more equipped we are with the skills needed for positive influence, the easier it will be to achieve our deepest desires in a healthy way that benefits many.

To continue to grow your level of influence, remember that it starts with small moments of persuasion. Don't tell people what to do, encourage them from personal experience and stories learned from others. Don't try and trick someone into doing the things they don't want to do. Be honest with reward and consequence so that they can properly make the decision for themselves.

Always ensure that you are reflecting on your own behavior to make sure that you aren't going about things in the wrong way. With becoming influential, there is a certain level of confidence that comes along as well. If you are not careful, that confidence will drive you too far ahead of others, and you can get lost in what you perceive to be best for everyone. The better you can reflect and ensure you have the right intention, the easier it will be for others to be legitimately inspired by you.

While it might be hard to do the right thing in times where what is easiest will also benefit you the most, remember to be empathetic towards others. Though it might be challenging, you will still ultimately get the things you desire most when you are doing so in a fair and rewarding way.